$ecrets of Power $alary Negotiating

Inside Secrets From a Master Negotiator

By

ROGER DAWSON

Franklin Lakes, NJ

SECRETS OF POWER SALARY NEGOTIATING
EDITED BY JODI BRANDON
TYPESET BY EILEEN DOW MUNSON
Cover design by Johnson Design
Printed in the U.S.A. by Book-mart Press

To order this title, please call toll-free 1-800-CAREER-1 (NJ and Canada: 201-848-0310) to order using VISA or MasterCard, or for further information on books from Career Press.

The Career Press, Inc., 3 Tice Road, PO Box 687,
Franklin Lakes, NJ 07417
www.careerpress.com

Library of Congress Cataloging-in-Publication Data

Dawson, Roger, 1940-
Secrets of power salary negotiating : inside secrets from a master negotiator / by Roger Dawson.
p. cm.
ISBN-13: 978-1-56414-860-5 (paper)
ISBN-10: 1-56414-860-2 (paper)
1. Employment interviewing. 2. Wages. 3. Negotiation. 4. Job hunting. I. Title.

HF5549.5.I6D39 2006
650.14´4—dc22

2005058102

Dedication ▸▸▸

To all the fine employers who value their employees and are eager to pay them what they are worth.

To all my seminar attendees who have shared their salary negotiation stories with me over the years.

To the human resource directors who shared their expertise with me but preferred to remain anonymous.

To the love of my life,
my wife Gisela.

To my three amazing children,
Julia, Dwight, and John.

To my two brilliant grandchildren,
Astrid and Thomas.

Portions of this book were previously published in *Secrets of Power Negotiating* and *Secrets of Power Negotiating for Salespeople* (both published by Career Press) and are used with the permission of the publisher.

Contents

Part Four: Closing Tactics 65

Section II: Negotiating Compensation, 105

Preface

What You'll Get From This Book

If you're an employee and you bought this book to learn some tricks to get your employer to pay you more than you're worth, you're going to be a mite disappointed. Yes, I'll teach you how to gain power in a negotiation, and I'll teach you some negotiating techniques that will get your employer (or potential employer) to pay you what you're worth, but I do not intend to tell you how you can get your employer to pay you more than you're worth. That, after all, would disrupt the sensitive fabric of capitalism as we know it.

If you're an employer who bought this book hoping to learn how to keep your employees slaving away at the modern equivalent of a salt mine for less than they are worth, you, too, are going to be disappointed.

What I believe is that many employees are working for far less than they are worth simply because they don't know how to negotiate a salary, and many employers could get far more from their employees if they knew how to negotiate compensation packages that would stimulate their employees to produce more.

More than any other negotiation, a salary negotiation must be win-win. Both sides must be genuinely happy with the result. Anything less and the arrangement will fall apart one day and both sides will be unhappy. A good salary negotiation should stimulate the employee to do his or her best while making huge profits for his or her employer.

That's what I will teach you in this book.

The book is divided into two sections:

In Section I: Getting the Offer, you'll learn how to:

- ▷ Write a resume that will get you an interview.
- ▷ Find the job openings.
- ▷ Interview well for the job.
- ▷ Get the employer to put an offer on the table, and learn how to respond to the offer.
- ▷ Use Closing Tactics to get a decision from the employer.

In Section II: Negotiating Compensation, you'll learn how to:

- ▷ Prepare for the negotiation.
- ▷ Use pressure points to improve the offer.
- ▷ Use Power Negotiating Gambits to get a compensation package.

If you already have a job offer, or if you're negotiating an increase in your present job, you can cut to the chase and go right to ***Section II: Negotiating Compensation.*** If you're looking for work or thinking about making a move, you should start with ***Section I: Getting the Offer.***

I promise you that by the time you finish this book, you'll have everything you'll ever need to get a great pay raise from your present employer or negotiate a dynamite compensation package from a new employer!

Roger Dawson
La Habra Heights, California

Introduction

I've been preaching for years that you cannot make money faster than you can when you're negotiating. When you're negotiating, figure out how long it took you to get a concession, and then multiply that out to a per-hour earning basis. Let's say that you spend an extra five minutes negotiating and you save yourself only $100. You spent five minutes to make $100, which means that you were making money at the rate of $1,200 per hour while you were negotiating. That's more than $2.3 million a year if you only worked 40 hours a week and took a four-week vacation! That's pretty good money! You cannot make money faster than you can when you're negotiating! A member of my golf club was once listed in the *Guinness Book of World Records* as the world's highest-paid heart surgeon, but even he would tell you that he makes more money per hour when he's negotiating a business deal.

This is even more true when you're negotiating an increase in pay, and here's why. There isn't a person in this country who couldn't walk into his or her boss's office and negotiate a $10 a week increase in pay. But that doesn't sound like very much does it? However, $10 a week is $520 a year. If you're with the company for another five years, that's $2,600 you just negotiated in increased compensation! And it probably only took you 15 minutes to do it—$2,600 in 15 minutes! That means that you were earning money at the rate of $10,400 per hour while you were negotiating that tiny increase in pay. Do you realize that, to be earning that kind of money, you'd have to be making nearly $20 million a year? There are only a handful of people in the world who are making that kind of money. Negotiating an increase in pay with your boss really is the highest and best use of your time. It's well worth taking some time to plan, to study, and to do it right. That's what I'll teach you in this book.

Section I

Getting the Offer

Part One

Resumes—Getting an Interview

Stage one of a salary negotiation is submitting a resume to the potential employer. Be very clear in your mind that the purpose of the resume is to get an interview. You cannot sell yourself to the employer with a resume. You cannot get the employer to make you an offer with a resume. The only thing a resume is good for is to get you to the next stage of the salary negotiation, which is the face-to-face interview.

Millions of resumes are submitted every day in this country—sent by mail, faxed, and e-mail. Where do they all go? Which ones does the employer even read? If an employer advertises a job, 500 to 2,000 resumes might be submitted. How can you make yours mean something? In this section you'll learn how to prepare your resume and how to get it read.

Chapter 1 ▶▶▶

Preparing the Resume

Things to Exclude From Your Resume

If you haven't applied for a job for a long while, you may not be aware that anything that could be considered discriminatory is a no-no in today's politically correct world. Employers are not allowed to ask your age, sex, marital status, religion, height, weight, or whether you smoke, and you're not to offer that information. The person who reviews your resume will immediately exclude you if you do. For one thing it shows that you're hopelessly out of touch, and for another it smells of an attorney trolling for a discrimination lawsuit.

How to Increase Your Chances of Getting Your Resume Read

The key issue is to make it relevant to the job for which you're applying. It's better to send 10 resumes that are tailored to the job than 100 resumes broadsided in the hope that one of them will attract attention. Remember that the HR director may be reviewing 50 or 60 resumes a day—perhaps more if the company accepts e-mail resumes. They are looking for ways to eliminate applicants at that stage. Lack of relevant background will get you kicked out. If you have tailored your resume to the job opening, the initial response may well be, "This could be just the person we're looking for. Let's get this one in for an interview."

The Optimum Length of a Good Resume

Consider the way that editors train their journalists to write stories: an attention-grabbing headline to make the reader want to read it, and a concise and interesting first paragraph that clearly states what the story is about. From then on, the story grows and expands with detail. You don't have to read it all to understand what it's about, but if the article continues to hold the reader's interest, they will read it to the end. Use the same formula when you're writing your resume. Your resume should scream, "I can solve your problems for you!" Use an attention-grabbing headline that is directly relevant to the job opening. Include a well-written description of your experience, starting with your most recent position and work back in time.

Don't let anyone tell you that a long resume is a mistake. A long resume is only a mistake if it's boring. If it continues to grab the interviewer's attention, it can be several pages long. A long resume is fine as long as the employer can pick it up and quickly see what he or she needs to know about the applicant. Long resumes are a big mistake when the employer tries to get to the crux of the applicants qualifications, but can't.

Some people write resumes with such gravitas that they think the employer will be so excited to get their resume that they will clear their desk to concentrate on reading it, and then call a hiring committee meeting to consider it. A more realistic approach would be to think of an employer groaning as he or she plows through a stack of 200 resumes. Your first challenge is to have your resume grab his or her attention.

Following Up After Sending the Resume

Should you call the employer after sending the resume? Only if you want to get hired! Call three days after sending the resume. Don't call to ask if they got it. That's lame, and if they have a stack of 200 resumes on their desk they probably won't know anyway. Remember that the purpose of your call is to get to the next level, which is the first interview. They're not going to hire you from a phone call, so don't even try to get hired. Focus on getting the interview. Use the lively "I can solve your problem" approach: "If you need someone to open up that territory in Alaska, I'm the perfect person for you. That's exactly what I did for my last company, and sales were 320 percent over budget. When can we get together? Would Wednesday or Thursday be better for you?" If you can't get an interview with this call, tell them that you'll call again in three days—and be sure that you do it.

Should You Include a Picture With Your Resume?

Use good judgment on this. If you think it will help, include a picture. If you have any reason to think it would be a negative, leave it out. Be sure that the picture is businesslike. No cheesecake. No vacation shots or jumping-out-of-a-plane shots.

Once they have interviewed you, the rules change. Include your picture on everything so they can recall you better. It's very easy to insert a small picture under your signature in a computer-generated letter.

Mistakes in Resume Preparation

1. The number one mistake is that your resume doesn't directly address the employer's needs, because you have submitted the same resume that you've sent to 200 other employers. What's so hard about customizing your resume to the job opening when you're doing it on a computer?

2. The second mistake is that the resume is confusing to read because it's loaded with technical jargon. Don't ask someone with a master's degree to review it; ask your friend who flunked out of high school. If he or she can figure out what job you're applying for, you're on the right track.
3. The third error is that it has spelling or grammatical errors. Every HR director I interviewed told me that they're surprised that they constantly get resumes with blatant grammatical errors and obvious spelling mistakes. How hard is it to use a spell and grammar checker? They conclude that some applicants don't even read their own resumes or cover letters before they send them off. If the resume is too dull for the applicant to read, how does he or she expect the employer to be thrilled?

Tailor Your Style to the Job Opening

If you're applying for a job as a sales manager at a used car superstore, you wouldn't use the same writing style as someone applying for a job as operations manager at a nuclear power plant. The sales manager might want to start with a blaring headline such as, "You want to move 200 cars a day?! I'm the one you need!" The operations manager approach would be much more low key—for example, "Experienced, qualified, calm as a rock under pressure."

If you're experienced in your profession or occupation you'll know the approach that will best please the employer.

Don't Forget to Include...

There are some important elements that you might forget to include, but could be critical in landing you that interview.

- ▷ **Computer competency.** Just about any job requires knowledge of computers and computer software these days, to say nothing of Blackberries and MP3s, so be sure to tout the equipment you can use and the software with which you're comfortable. Of course, if you're certified by one of the software manufacturers, such as MCSE (Microsoft Certified Systems Engineer), CCNA (Cisco Certified Networking Associate), CNE (Novell Certified NetWare Engineer), or CAN (Novell Certified NetWare Administrator), you'll want to feature these valuable credentials.

- **Charitable work.** Volunteerism is big these days, so be sure to mention the Habitat for Humanity that you've helped build, the soup kitchens at which you've served, the golf tournaments you've run, and the money you've collected for charity.
- **Foreign languages.** The global village is here, and it's hard to think of a company that doesn't have some business overseas, so let employers know if you speak any foreign languages. Knowledge of Japanese or Mandarin could be a job cincher.

A Surefire Way to Get an Interview

Here is a great idea when you are having trouble getting the employer to grant you a first interview. My old friend Tim Rush taught me this one. It has four stages to it, and I'll be surprised if you get to stage four without getting an interview even with the most recalcitrant HR director.

- **Stage One:** Type up a brief introduction letter that says, "In a very big way I think I can do a terrific job for you." Take it down to Kinko's or your local print shop and have them blow it up into a 2-foot by 3-foot poster. Wrap it up and mail it to the HR director.

- ▷ **Stage Two:** Get an old shoe and mail it to them with a big card enclosed that says, "Now that I've got my foot in the door, I'd like an opportunity to tell you what I can do for you." One warning here. Don't do this if the recipient is Arab, Persian or Thai. Showing the bottom of your foot to these people can be very insulting. In that case, skip Stage Two and go to Stage Three.
- ▷ **Stage Three:** Buy a hammer at the 99-cent store and put it in a box with a big card that says, "I'd like to drive home the point that I'm the perfect person for the job."
- ▷ **Stage Four:** Buy a small gardening spade and box it up with a note that says, "Why don't you dig my resume out from that big stack on your desk and give me a call?"

If that doesn't work, send a note that says, "I've been trying to get my foot in your door for two weeks now. At least I managed to get my shoe in the door. Now will you let me hobble in for an interview and give me my shoe back?" If the HR director has any sense of humor at all, he or she will admire your creativity and grant you the interview long before you get to this stage.

Key Points to Consider:

- The purpose of a resume is to get you a face-to-face interview. Nothing more.
- Leave out any information that could be discriminatory. Employers are not allowed to ask your age, sex, marital status, religion, height, weight, or whether you smoke (and you're not to offer that information).

- Make your resume directly relevant to the job being offered.
- A long resume is okay as long as the important information is upfront. Model your opening after a good, attention-grabbing headline in a newspaper, and then expand on the story later in the resume.
- Imagine that the reader is reviewing a stack of 200 resumes. What in your resume makes him or her pick up the phone and call you in for an interview?
- Follow up with a phone call within three days.
- Use the "I can solve your problem" approach.
- Triple-check your spelling and grammar. With today's computer software, there is no excuse for errors.
- Tailor your style of writing to the job opening.
- Be creative in your attempts to get a face-to-face interview!

Part Two

The Interview—Getting a Job Offer

Stage two of a salary negotiation is the interview. The purpose of the interview, from your point of view, is to get the potential employer to make an offer. Be sure that you focus on this objective. At no time during the interview should you even suggest that money is an issue. You should only start to negotiate the amount of your compensation package once you have a firm offer from the employer.

The first interview is one of the scariest things about getting a new job. You're going into unknown territory. You may have only done this a few times in your life, and you'll be dealing with someone who does it 10 or more times a day. You're intimidated because there is a lot of reward and punishment power in play here. You could come out of this with the perfect job with a fabulous compensation package. This could be something that will positively affect your life for the next 20 years! On the other side, it could end in total humiliation. You might be completely unqualified for the job and they may laugh at your salary request. No wonder you're intimidated!

My golfing buddy Ted Petropoulis tells the story of being on a hiring panel for the local police department. A woman applied for the job who clearly had absolutely no qualifications. They were polite to her, but Ted finally asked her, "Could I ask you why you applied for this job when you have no experience or qualifications?" The applicant rolled her eyes and said, "Well, sir, it's like this. When you see a gravy train going by, you just naturally want to jump on it!"

Chapter 2 ▸▸▸ Gathering Information About the Company

Using the Internet to Find Job Openings

The *Wall Street Journal* has an excellent site intended for college graduates (*www.college.wsj.com*). Do a keyword search for "chemist," for example, and you get 29 job openings around the country. You get specific employers and locations and you can click through to apply for the job online.

The granddaddy of job search Websites is Monster (*www.Monster.com*). If you enter "chemist" at that site, you find 987 job openings.

If sticking your head in the federal government trough appeals to you, try *jobsearch.usajobs.opm.gov/index.asp*, which has 81 openings for chemists. If you want to find out what a federal job pays, find out the **grade** and the **step** and go to *www.opm.gov*. Click on "General Schedule and Locality Pay Tables." It's written in government-speak, but you should be able to figure it out.

The federal government offers a massive Website from the Bureau of Labor Statistics (*www.bls.gov*). Getting information from this site can be thought of as taking a sip of water from a fire hose, but it's all in there somewhere. You're paying for it—or at least you will be when you find a job and start paying taxes, so you might as well use it.

Learning More About the Company

Learning more used to be hard work, but with the Internet it's easy:

- Thoroughly read the company's Website. Find it by going to Google (*www.google.com*) and type in the company name. Be sure to read the press release section so that you're up on current events at the company. It makes you appear so informed to be able to say, "Didn't you open a new assembly plant in Bangladesh last month?"
- Look the company up at the Standard and Poor's Website (*www.standardandpoors.com*). This is a McGraw-Hill company that researches companies and sells the information to subscribers, but it gives a lot of free information about companies on its Website.
- Use Hoovers (*www.hoovers.com*) to research the company. This is a Dunn and Bradstreet company that sells information to subscribers, but it also offers a lot of free information on its Website.

Key Points to Consider:

- Use the Internet to learn everything you can about the company.
- If you're graduating from college, check out *www.college.wsj.com.* It's the *Wall Street Journal* job-opening site for college graduates.
- Monster (*www.monster.com.*) is the biggest job search site.
- If working for the federal government appeals to you, go to *www.usajobs.gov.* (You can find Federal pay grades at *www.opm.gov.*)

- Research a company by going through Google (*www.google.com*). Put in the company name and hit "I feel lucky." Be sure to research the press release section for current company news.
- Go to Standard and Poor's (*www.standardandpoors.com*) to check what it has to say about a company. It's a portal for an expensive subscription service, but you can learn a lot about a company without charge.
- Dunn and Bradsheet's opinion of a company can be found at *www.hoovers.com*. Again, it's a portal site, but you can learn a lot without paying.

Chapter 3 ▸▸▸

Preparing for the Interview

As is the case with anything else, the more prepared you are for the interview, the more relaxed you will be, and the better you will do. Preparation is the key. I remember when I did my first (and last) parachute jump, I was absolutely terrified when I showed up at the jump zone in the morning, but after a few hours of having them show me the equipment and jumping off higher and higher platforms, I had enough confidence to get on the plane—I was still terrified, but at least I had my fear under control.

Contrast that with a time when I went scuba diving in St. Thomas, Virgin Islands. I went with a group from a cruise ship, who were nearly all first-timers. By law, they had to take a short class to qualify them to dive. When we arrived at the dive shop, their classroom was full, so our instructor said, "Never mind, I'll teach you on the way down to the beach." He loaded us onto an open-sided bus and, as it roared around the curves to the beach, he stood in front of us holding up the equipment and yelling instructions to us. It was totally inadequate. As you can imagine, the dive was a nightmare. Most of the would-be-divers panicked before they got their shoulders underwater and only a handful of us completed the dive, even though we were only in shallow water. Preparation is the key to overcoming fear and building self-confidence.

It's a good idea to go on a few interviews for jobs that you don't care about, just to develop some confidence. This will help you get a feel for how it goes and what to expect.

Rehearsing for the Interview

If you're worried that the HR director will throw a question at you that you won't feel comfortable answering, it's a good idea to rehearse the answers to questions that might rattle you. Think of yourself as a nominee for the Supreme Court who is preparing for your grilling by the Senate judicial committee. Have your significant other play the role of a hostile HR director and fire the tough questions at you. You'll be much better prepared for the actual interview. Remember that if the interviewer is sitting there looking at your resume he or she is not going to ask you questions that you've already answered in writing. Try to think of questions that are not covered. Here are some that you might be asked:

- ▷ Tell me about the challenges that you faced on this job. *You are almost certain to be asked this, so prepare a story for each job you've had. Rehearse the problem and tell how you took control and came through shining.*
- ▷ How much do you expect to get paid? *I'll help you with this question a little later in this section.*
- ▷ Would you take less?
- ▷ Why did you leave your former employer?
- ▷ What do you want to do for us?
- ▷ Have you ever refused to do something because you thought it was unethical?
- ▷ On this job, who did you have the most problem getting along with?
- ▷ What are your strengths?
- ▷ What are your weaknesses?
- ▷ What would you do if a person who reported to you refused to follow your instructions?
- ▷ Why didn't you finish college?

- What are you most proud of?
- May I check with your current employer?
- I'm concerned that you don't have enough experience handling ______.

Remember that your first interview will probably be by telephone. An assistant to the HR director will call you out of the blue and ask you some qualifying questions. The objective at this stage is to narrow the list of applicants, so he or she will be looking for issues that could disqualify you. Your objective is to keep your resume in the stack of potential hires and move to the next level, which is the first face-to-face interview. Stay focused on that with direct appeals: "When can I come in to see you?" or "What do I have to do to get an interview?"

What Is the Interviewer Trying to Find Out?

Interviewers want to learn three things about you:

1. That you can solve their problem by handling the opening they have to fill. Your strategy should be to find out all you can about this specific job opening and what you would be doing for the company. Tailor your approach to that opportunity, but also leave open the possibility that they will love you so much that they'll find another place for you in the company if the current opening is filled.
2. That you have leadership skills and can inspire and motivate people to work harder and accomplish more. Your strategy should be to tell a colorful story about the time you took over in an emergency and became the company hero with your initiative, drive, creativity, and daring leadership skills.
3. You will fit in with their corporate culture. Your strategy should be to talk about the company softball team that you captained. Be sure that you treat

everyone you meet at the new company as if he or she is the most important person you'll meet that day. You can't ride roughshod over the personnel secretary and ingratiate yourself with the interviewer. They compare notes after you leave, you know.

How to Stand Out at an Interview When There Are a Lot of Applicants

Most applicants will dutifully answer all the questions that they are asked and hope they get a job offer. This is not a good negotiating strategy. You want to come across as a highly desirable applicant who will be choosing from a myriad of offers. As I'll explain later in Section Two: "Negotiating Compensation," options give you power in a negotiation. A good way to project that you have options is to take some time at the end of the interview to see if the employer can offer you what you expect. After the interviewer has asked you her questions, you ask your questions. They might include:

- Who are your major competitors, and why are you better than them?
- What is your corporate mission statement?
- Do you try to promote from within?
- Where do you think this company will be five years from now?
- Are you prepared to make an offer today?
- When will I hear from you?

Asking questions projects that you're not going to jump at the first job offered you and that you have several options, which gives you power in the subsequent salary negotiation.

How to Stress Your Skills in an Interview

You need to express your skills as benefits to the employer. Salespeople know the difference between features of the product they are selling and the benefits of owning the product. "These roofing tiles are made of concrete" is a feature. "So they'll never catch fire, blow away, or wear out" are the benefits.

In an employment interview, "I'm an experienced negotiator. At my last job at the leasing company I bought more than 8,000 cars a year" is a feature. "I saved the company more than $122,000 last year over what they were paying for the cars before they hired me," is a benefit.

How to Keep the Interview Process Moving Forward

Be sure that you send the interviewer a handwritten thank-you note. That's what makes you stand out from all the other people he or she interviewed that day. Don't be tempted to type a formal letter, because a handwritten note is much more powerful. Be sure to personalize it with a comment about something that happened during the interview. The perfect vehicle is a postcard that has your picture on it. Your picture reminds the interviewer of who you are and, because it's not in an envelope, there's no danger that a secretary will open the envelope and discard the letter.

Sending a thank-you note in this way indicates that you're a caring, people person. Because nearly all HR directors are caring, people persons, they will like you for it. It also shows how organized you are and how much you'd like to work with them.

Send a thank-you card to everyone with whom you came in contact at the company, not just the people who you feel could help or hire you.

Follow up your handwritten note with a brief e-mail. Having your e-mail address at hand makes it much easier for the interviewer to reply to you.

Key Points to Consider:

- Preparation is the key to overcoming fear and building self-confidence. Practice! Practice! Practice!
- First go on a few interviews for jobs that you don't care about, just to develop some confidence. Get a feel for how it goes and what to expect.
- Role-play with a friend and have him or her fire questions at you from the list in this chapter.
- A preliminary telephone interview from an assistant is a "screening-out" interview. Your objective is to stay in the game and get a face-to-face interview. Stay focused on that with direct appeals: "When can I come in to see you?" or "What do I have to do to get an interview?"
- Interviewers want to hear three things:
  1. That you can solve their problem.
  2. That you can inspire and motivate other people.
  3. That you will fit their corporate culture.
- End the interview by interviewing the company. Asking penetrating questions about what the company can offer you projects that you have many options, which gives you power in the subsequent salary negotiation.
- Don't just stress your skills; translate those skills into benefits for the company. For example, you might say, "I have excellent public speaking skills so I'll be able to help you train your people."
- Follow up the interview with a handwritten (not typed) note that includes your picture. Then send a thank-you e-mail so that the HR director can easily reply to you.

Chapter 4 ▶▶▶

Handling the Issue of Money

This is the most delicate issue to be raised in a negotiation. Employers will try to raise this issue early in the process because they don't want to waste time on applicants they can't afford. Also, they want to make your past earnings a big issue because they think it will lower your salary expectations. You want to delay the discussion of money as long as you possibly can—until they are convinced that you're the person they need. That way you'll get a better offer.

Here are some tips on how to handle this sensitive issue.

What to Say When Asked "What You Are Getting Paid Now?"

Try not to answer this question until they are drooling to get you on board, but if forced to answer, be sure that you include all your benefits, not just your salary. Your response should be, "I feel that my total package is worth about $80,000 a year." Your way of calculating that would include:

- Base salary.
- Bonuses, both actual and potential.
- Vacation pay.
- Stock options.
- Travel allowances.
- Health plans.
- Life insurance.

- ▷ Access to company health club.
- ▷ Employee discounts.
- ▷ The benefits of not having a long commute to work.
- ▷ Reimbursement for meals.
- ▷ Frequent flyer points collected.
- ▷ Hotel frequent guest points collected.
- ▷ Reimbursement for tuition.
- ▷ Training given by company beyond that of learning about the company.
- ▷ Retirement plans.
- ▷ 401(k) contributions.
- ▷ Free cappuccino machine in the lunchroom. (That's two cups a day, which would be $3 each at Starbucks, for 250 working days in the year. That's $1,500 right there!)

As you can see, there is a huge difference between your base salary and your total compensation package. If you were to respond to their question about current earnings by just giving them your base salary, you would be vastly underrating yourself.

What to Do if You Get a Low Offer for a Job

Write them a sincere counter-offer letter or, better yet, call and ask for an appointment to discuss a counter-offer. Negotiations always work better face-to-face for several reasons:

- ▷ You can read the body language better face-to-face.
- ▷ You can communicate your seriousness better.
- ▷ You can shake hands and reach an agreement on the spot.

If you are reduced to writing a letter, make these points:

- ▷ You sincerely admire the company, see great opportunity there, and want to work for them. The only stumbling block is the compensation.
- ▷ Restate all the great things you could do in the position.
- ▷ Mention that you have another offer available to you that pays more, but you really want to go with this company. Projecting that you have options gives you power. It also makes it easier for the HR director to sell his or her boss on paying you more.
- ▷ Ask for more than you expect to get so they can have a win with you. Imply some flexibility to encourage them to negotiate with you. Perhaps you could say, "I really feel that I'm well worth $100,000. I might take a *little* less."
- ▷ Support your requested amount with research that justifies it.
- ▷ List the items on which you have reached agreement. It reminds the HR director of all the work he's gone through to get this far. He is then more likely to be flexible because he subconsciously wants to recoup the time already invested.

Once You Have Agreed on a Package, Ask for It in Writing

Is it appropriate to ask for the offer in writing? Yes, by all means. Your new employer wants to eliminate any misunderstandings just as much as you do. Get it in writing and be sure that the letter includes all of the details. If it's a high-level position, try to get it signed by an officer of the company.

Key Points to Consider:

- Try not to answer the question of how much you're making currently until the employer is drooling to get you on board. If forced to respond, quote the value of your total package including all benefits.
- If the employer makes a low offer, try to get an appointment to discuss it so that you can negotiate face-to-face.
- When negotiating, let the employer know that you have options. Ask for more than you expect to get, but imply some flexibility to encourage the employer to negotiate.
- Once you've reached an agreement, ask for it in writing so there are no misunderstandings.

Chapter 5 ▸▸▸

What the Interviewer Is Looking For

What impresses an HR director? What is he or she looking for in an applicant? If she has several applicants with similar credentials, what would make her pick you? Here are eight key issues that give you an edge over other applicants:

1. Credentials.
2. Reward Power.
3. Punishment Power.
4. Consistency.
5. Character.
6. Charisma.
7. Expertise Power.
8. Information Power.

Credentials

In the United States we are influenced by titles. Not as much as in Germany or Switzerland, but we're high on the list of countries where a title gives status. If you've had titles in high school, college, or previous employment, be sure to mention them, because titles build your credentials. Anything you can do to stress your credentials is valuable. They might include:

- ▷ High school and college degrees. Include any leadership roles that you took in campus activities.
- ▷ Scholastic achievements.

- ▷ Titles in previous jobs. Have you been a vice president, a sales manager, or a group leader on a project?
- ▷ Recognition by industry peers. Have you been president of your industry association, on the board of directors, or on a committee? Have you received any rewards from your industry association, such as member of the year?

Also, specific experience gives you major credentials. Have you put out oil fires in Kuwait or built bridges in Brazil?

Reward Power

What can you tell the interviewer that emphasizes the problems that you solve for him, and the money you can make for him? This is a big one, and you need to pour it on. The belief that you can solve problems and build his business is what builds the excitement to get you on the payroll. Be specific about how much money your accomplishments made for your previous employers.

Punishment Power

This is much harder to do without causing offense. But if there is a way that you can convince them of the problems that they could get into if they don't hire you, it is a powerful point to make. Perhaps you can say something such as, "This type of work is very complicated. It takes a lot of skill to get it right and the downside of not doing it well is enormous."

Consistency

Trust is a product of consistency. If you want the employer to trust you, which is essential, you must project consistency. For example, it's okay to have made several job moves, as long as each one was to better yourself or gain the experience you'd need to build a career. However, if you've flopped around from one job to another without any sense of purpose, that's bad.

HR directors love to hear that you've had a passion for your field ever since grade school. They don't like students who took a liberal arts course because they couldn't decide what to do with their lives, and have switched from job to job trying to find something that interested them.

Character

The interviewer will no doubt be looking for indications of high moral character. Be careful that you don't drop your standards just to please. If the interviewer asks you if you could quit your present job and start right away, your response should be, "I think that my present employer would agree to that, but if not I would feel obligated to give them two weeks' notice. They have been so good to me." Be careful that you are not in any way implying that you could bring company secrets with you or help them recruit your present company's employees.

Charisma

Projecting charisma makes a big difference. I cover this at length in my book *Secrets of Power Persuasion* (Prentice-Hall), but here are some brief tips:

▷ **Handshake.** This is important because it's the first physical contact with the interviewer. Ask a good friend to coach you on improving your handshake. Shake hands and ask him or her to rate your handshake on a scale of one to 10. Then ask what it would take to get it to a 10. If you're a gripper, a pumper, or a wet fish, you need to work on your handshake.

- ▷ **Eye contact.** As you shake hands notice the color of the interviewer's eyes and silently count to three. Holding of his or her gaze for a little longer than you otherwise would makes a big impression.
- ▷ **Push out a warm thought.** As you shake the interviewer's hand and look deeply into his or her eyes, push out a warm, positive thought, such as, "I'm really glad that I met you; this is going to be the start of a long friendship."
- ▷ **Smile** as you shake hands and again as you sit down to talk. You may be feeling very nervous, but it won't show if you are wearing a big smile.

Charisma is very hard to explain. We know it when we see it, but we have trouble explaining it. When you are having trouble understanding something, it helps to think of the opposite. What characteristics would you ascribe to the least charismatic person on earth? With whom would you least like to spend the rest of your life on a desert island? I think it would be a person who is totally self-centered, someone who only thinks of him or herself.

Take John Paul Getty, for example. When he was the richest man in the world, many people wanted to own what he owned, but nobody wanted to be who he was. Aristotle Onassis had the greatest difficulty in doing business with him until, as he explains in his autobiography, he accepted that anything Getty would do would be totally self serving.

If the opposite of charisma is being self-centered, it becomes clear that charisma is the ability to project that you care about every one with whom you come in contact. You don't have to be a Mother Theresa, caring about every poor person on the planet, or a Martin Luther King, caring about everyone suffering racial injustice, but you do need to care about everyone you meet.

Dale Carnegie had some great advice in this regard. He said, "Treat everyone you meet as if they are the most important person you'll meet that day." That's well said, isn't it? Not the most important person you'll ever meet or even the most important person you'll meet that week—that would be over the top. Treat everyone you meet as if they were the most important person you'll meet that day. You can't get away with treating the HR director with respect while treating the secretary as a servant.

Expertise Power

This is more important than ever in today's high-tech world, isn't it? If you have an expertise that this company needs, you develop a great deal of power over it. There is a famous story about IBM when it had a very strict dress code. Everyone wore gray suits and white, button-down-collar shirts. An executive was visiting a regional office and rode up in the elevator with a scruffy looking man wearing sandals, blue jeans, and a t-shirt. He was horrified and berated the manager for not enforcing the dress code for visitors. The manager told him that the man wasn't a visitor; he was an employee. "Not any more," said the executive. "Fire him!" They fired him but quickly had to rehire him, sandals and all, when they realized that he had a programming expertise nobody else had.

Be sure that you're projecting expertise during the interview. That's why it's so important to tell stories of the challenges that you faced on previous assignments and how you overcame those challenges.

Information Power

Human beings have a tremendous natural curiosity. That may have killed the cat, but curiosity made us masters of the universe. We can't stand not knowing. You can put a cow in a field and it will stay in that field all its life, never wondering what's on the other side of that hill. But humans are going to spend billions of dollars to fly to Mars because we have to know if there's microscopic life there or not.

HR directors love to hear inside secrets of how things are at other companies. You mustn't give away any company secrets, of course, but they love to hear stories of the corporate executives you've met and the personnel activities you attended.

Key Points to Consider:

Stress these keys points in an interview. They are what the HR director is looking for:

- Any title that you've held, because titles build credibility.
- How you can solve problems for him or her.
- How you avoid problems for him or her.
- Consistency in your career path and career goals.
- Maintain the highest moral standards. Don't imply that you will bring company secrets with you or help them recruit from your old company.
- Study the tips I gave you for increasing your charisma.
- Most important, stress any areas of expertise that other applicants may not have.

Chapter 6 ▸▸▸

Problem Issues

What to Do if Your Previous Employer Won't Give a Good Reference

First, you should confirm your suspicions. Is your previous company really badmouthing you, or has your paranoia overwhelmed you? To find out, have a friend call the old employee as if he or she were a personnel clerk for a new employer. Just have him or her call the personnel department and see how much information the old employer will give out. Your friend should keep asking questions until the personnel department shuts him or her up. We live in such a litigious age that few employers will give out negative information. They will limit themselves to confirming the dates worked and will possibly respond negatively if asked the question, "Would you rehire?" They will almost never confirm earnings, because they don't want their current employees nosing around.

When I was a personnel director I would only give out dates of employment and a terse "no comment" to the "would you rehire" question. Once I was so upset with an employee that had unjustly sued us that I asked to return the call, to be sure that I wasn't talking to an attorney, and then said, "I have a policy that if I can't say anything nice about someone I won't say anything at all." That's as nasty as I ever got.

Remember that if you are claiming unemployment insurance, the old employer has a vested interest in getting you off of its State claim list.

What to Do if You've Been Unemployed for a Long Time

Here are some suggestions to help handle this sensitive situation:

- ▷ "I've been doing some consulting work. Being self-employed appealed to me for a while, but now I realize that I can't reach my full potential unless I'm with a big company."
- ▷ "I left to do some traveling that was important to me, but I've got it out of my system now."
- ▷ "I left my last job a year ago because I couldn't achieve my full potential and I've treated my job search as a full-time job. I've had several offers, but I'm prepared to wait until I find the perfect opportunity."
- ▷ "We felt that it was important for one of us to stay home until our child went into kindergarten."
- ▷ "My father was ill and I needed to be with him."

Don't lie, of course, but realize that taking a year off from work makes a lot of sense to some people. Don't think of it as something to be ashamed off. Taking a year off from work is something about which most Americans dream.

What to Do if You Were Fired From Your Last Job

There is no need to tie yourself up in knots over this issue. Everybody on the planet has been fired from a job at one time or another. The interviewer will be far more interested in *why* you were fired from the job. Let's take a look at some acceptable reasons for being fired:

- ▷ They downsized and I didn't have the seniority to make the cut.

- ▷ They closed at that location and I was not willing to move.
- ▷ They outsourced my job to India.

Now here are some unacceptable reasons for being fired:

- ▷ They caught me stealing.
- ▷ I sued them for poor employment practices and I lost.
- ▷ My boss was an idiot and wouldn't listen to me.

Remember that they will probably only find out if you were fired if you tell them. The vast majority of previous employers will only verify the dates worked.

Key Points to Consider:

- Don't be too concerned that your former employer will give you a bad reference. Employers are so scared of lawsuits these days that they're not going to go out on a limb.
- Find out what kind of reference the previous employer will give by having a friend call for a reference.
- If you've been unemployed for a while, come up with a good reason for your sabbatical.

Part Three

Responding to the Offer

Stage three of a salary negotiation is responding to the offer. You now have an offer on the table and the ball is in your court. Is it a good offer? What more can you ask for? Let's consider those factors, and then we can move on to the actual negotiation.

When is the best time to start talking about what the job pays? Not until the company is ready to make you an offer, and even then you may be better off to defer the discussion of compensation. On the application where it asks you for expected salary write "Negotiable." If the interviewer presses you, say, "I'm sure that we can negotiate something that is mutually acceptable, but let's discuss that when we both feel that I'm right for the job."

The ideal time to bring this up is when the employer is drooling to hire you and thinks it'll lose you unless it makes you a great offer now. Remember the old-time encyclopedia salespeople who would come to your door? They would never give you the price until they had built your desire to own the encyclopedia. If they knocked on your door and said, "Do you want to buy a set of encyclopedias? They cost $700," they would never sell any. Build the desire for that employer to hire you. Build it to a fever pitch before you talk about compensation.

Chapter 7 ▸▸▸ What Can You Get?

Hiring Bonuses

Will companies pay a hiring bonus? Yes, this is a popular way to attract a good employee without the difficulties that can be caused internally by paying top wages to a new employee. Expect to be able to negotiate up to three months of base pay. The more you emphasize the bonus that you will be leaving behind at your current employer, the more chance you have of getting a hiring bonus. You will probably be asked to sign a statement that you will repay the bonus if you don't stay with the new company for 12 months. Don't worry about signing it, because the company knows it has almost no chance of getting the money back from you. You should give it back, of course, but it would be, to all intents and purposes, a voluntary act.

If you've negotiated all you can on salary, try getting a hiring bonus, a year-end bonus, or a 90-day review based on performance.

Severance Packages

Can you negotiate a severance package up front? It's possible, but not easy for a salaried employee. If you were in top management it would be much easier. If you have a severance package with your current employer, by all means ask your new employer to match it. If your new company is in play, you'd have a reason to say, "I'm concerned about corporate takeovers in this day and age. What protection will you give me in the event the company is sold and my position is eliminated?"

Because talking about leaving the company before you even start is a sensitive issue, an agent or attorney negotiating your compensation package for you is in a better position to handle this.

Companies Need to Make a Profit on You

Yes, you must accept that companies need to make more money from you than they pay you! That's thinking as a capitalist, and employers love you for it! You'd be amazed at how many young people entering the marketplace think that their employer is cheating them because they're making more money for their company than the company is paying them. Well, duh! Of course they have to make a profit on an employee; that's the way they stay in business.

Employees love to hear you say, "If you're going to pay me the $100,000 that I think I'm worth, I'll have to make about $500,000 a year for you so that we can both be happy. Let's talk about how I can do that for you."

Other Negotiable Factors

A whole bunch of things are negotiable, many of which get overlooked by focusing on the cash-in-hand benefits.

Let's start by looking at benefits:

- ▷ Insurance: health, dental, vision, disability, and life.
- ▷ Time off: sick days, personal days, paid holidays, vacation (how many days and how can they be taken), maternity/paternity leave.
- ▷ Travel: car-pooling, free parking, reimbursement per mile, bus or subway reimbursement.
- ▷ Professional advancement: training courses, attendance at association meetings, and reimbursement for travel and expenses, dues for membership in professional associations.

- ▷ Recreation: health club membership, golf club membership, access to company-owned facilities.
- ▷ Miscellaneous: discounts on company products and services, financial assistance with emergency loans.
- ▷ How will disputes be settled? By arbitration or legal action? Who will pay for this?

Now let's look at work-related issues:

- ▷ Size and location of office.
- ▷ Can you work from home using a company-supplied computer and high-speed Internet access?
- ▷ How flexible are your working hours?
- ▷ How quickly and how often will your compensation be reviewed?
- ▷ To whom will you report and who will report to you?

Other forms of compensation:

- ▷ Signing bonus, stock options, profit sharing, retirement plan, severance pay, and performance bonuses.

Relocation allowances:

- ▷ Is packing of furniture included in moving costs? What about days off and reimbursement for cost of house-hunting, bonus for move (such as a month's salary), selling costs for old home, buying costs for new home, and cost of spouse finding a new job?

As you can see, there are a myriad of things that can be overlooked. Decide before you go into final negotiations what you must have and what you're willing to give up or trade away for a higher salary.

When to Mention How Much You Expect

Should you raise the issue of compensation up front so that you're not wasting your time on a job that doesn't pay enough?

Absolutely not! Never raise the issue of compensation until the employer brings it up. For you to raise the issue would be confrontational and might be considered arrogant. However carefully you phrase the issue, it could well sound as though you're saying, "I've got better things to do if you can't afford to pay me what I think I'm worth."

What to Do if the Employer Insists on Knowing Your Salary History

Let's start with three rules about requests for salary history, assuming that you want to make much more than you have in the past:

1. Never offer to give information on past salary.
2. If asked, try to avoid answering with tactics such as:
    - "Let's hold off until we both feel that this is the right job for me."
    - "We can work that out later. Finding the right career path is far more important for me at this stage."
3. If forced to answer, don't lie (they could fire you for it later), but fog your response with:
    - "The total compensation package was around $95,000." Include in that estimate the value to you of every possible benefit.
    - "I accepted a low salary to get experience in that profession."
    - "Obviously I wouldn't work for that little today."

- "Remember, that was in Charleston, West Virginia. I'd need twice as much here in San Francisco."
- "At that time there were a lot of computer programmers looking for work, so salaries were severely depressed."
- "That's what they were paying me, but I was up for a huge raise just as I decided to make a career move to broaden my experience."

Key Points to Consider:

- A hiring bonus is a definite possibility. It's a way for the employer to recruit you without paying you more than it's paying its current employees.
- Don't be concerned about signing a promise to pay the hiring bonus back if you don't stay. The employer knows it can never collect.
- Stress the bonus that you'll be giving up if you leave your present employer now.
- Try for a year-end bonus and a salary review after 90 days.
- A severance package is a possibility, particularly if you're in top management, but it's a sensitive issue to discuss in a hiring interview. Save it for later.
- Employers need to make a profit off you! Stress how much you're going to make for them, and your compensation requests will seem more reasonable.
- Don't focus entirely on how much they're going to pay you. There are many other factors that can be valuable to you.
- Don't talk about former earnings. If you're forced to, have a reason for accepting an assignment that paid you less than you're worth.

Chapter 8 ▸▸▸
How Much Should You Ask For?

How Employers Decide on the Amount of an Offer

How does an employer decide how much to offer you? A Human Resources director at one of the biggest international companies in the world told me that his company uses three key factors:

1. What you made on your last job.
2. Surveys of the marketplace to determine what the competition is offering for similar jobs.
3. Internal equity. Would this offer be fair and in line with what current employees are being paid? If you're asking for more than the employer is currently paying its people, you should negotiate a one-time hiring bonus.

How to Calculate What the Job Is Worth

The Internet is a powerful source of information.

The Website *www.salary.com* has a comprehensive salary calculator. Let's say that I'm looking for a job as a commercial real estate appraiser and look at the site's alphabetical list of job titles. I find that number 9 is Appraiser (Commercial Real Estate). Its gives a description of the job as:

> *Responsible for the appraisal of residential and commercial properties. Investigates the fair*

market value and property ratings through analysis and inspection of properties. Ensures that the properties are in accordance with departmental specifications. Requires a bachelor's degree and at least 7 years of experience in the field or in a related area. Familiar with a variety of the field's concepts, practices, and procedures. Relies on experience and judgment to plan and accomplish goals. Performs a variety of tasks. May lead and direct the work of others. A wide degree of creativity and latitude is expected. Typically reports to a head of unit or department.

The site shows some suggested job titles:

- ▷ Appraisal Manager.
- ▷ Manager of Appraisal.
- ▷ Real Estate Appraisal Manager.

By clicking through with my zip code I find that the Webiste will give me a base salary and bonus without charging me a fee. I find that the median pay is $84,035. That means according to the site's survey of HR directors, half are paying more than that and half are paying less. It also shows me that if you add the median annual bonus it will bring total salary to $89,280.

Another great source is *www.salaryexpert.com.* By clicking on a profession (let's say cardiologist) and a city (Los Angeles), you quickly get a free report that shows you:

The Cardiologist working in Cypress, California now earns an average salary of $237,719. Half of those in this position would earn between $151,070 and $656,366 (the 17th and 67th percentiles). These numbers are derived from real, area specific, survey data. When benefits and bonuses are added to this salary, the average total compensation for this position would be $303,721.

Both of these services offer more comprehensive information for a small fee. Obviously, these reports can be of great value in a salary negotiation. When an employer makes you a low offer you can say, "I researched this on the Internet at *salary.com* and *salaryexpert.com,* and they indicated the medium salary was $15,000 more than that."

Calculating What College Graduates Are Worth

Go the Website *www.jobweb.com.* It offers a wealth of information for college graduates on job opportunities, expected salaries, and which professions are hot.

Calculating the Cost of Living at a New Location

The National Association of Realtors has a Website that will calculate an dcompare the cost of living for you. Go to *www.homefair.com.* Click on "The Salary Calculator," which is in the Research Calculators section. Enter the city that you're leaving and the city you're going to. For example, it will tell you that if you're making $100,000 a year in Charleston, South Carolina, you'll need to make $145,673 in Laguna Beach, California. That's a key issue in salary negotiations that involve a move, and it's a valid issue for which you should expect compensation.

Key Points to Consider:

- Employers make an offer based on three factors:
  1. How much you've made in the past.
  2. What other companies are paying.
  3. What the company currently pays its employees.

- Research salary levels at *www.salary.com* or *www.salaryexpert.com.*
- Find out what college graduates are worth at *www.jobweb.com.*
- If the job offer requires relocating, check out the compared costs of living at *www.homefair.com.*

Chapter 9 ▸▸▸ Leaving Your Present Job

Negotiating Severance After You Get Fired

You would have been better off to negotiate severance pay when you joined the company, but you still have some options available to you. Here are some suggestions:

- ▷ Check your state law. You many find that many things are mandated by law. (There are no federal laws about severance pay). Certainly the employer owes you for any work done, vacation time, and *perhaps* sick days that you haven't taken, but it may also be required to make health coverage portable. For example, a quick Google search told me that in my state, California, the law requires payment of unused vacation pay but not unused sick pay. There are no laws mandating severance pay in California.
- ▷ Don't be too discouraged if the state law doesn't help you. There are many other reasons for your company to offer you severance pay other than that it's mandated:
  - A simple attitude of fairness and appreciation for the work you've done.
  - The employer wants you to speak well of the company.

- The employer doesn't want the hassle of a lawsuit claiming that it discriminated against you.
- The employer doesn't want you stealing employees to go with you to your next company.
- The employer might pay you for a promise not to go with a competitor.

Don't sign anything unless you have reviewed it carefully when you were not under emotional stress. You may be signing away some valuable rights in the heat of the moment. It may look generous, but if the employer is buying you off because you were fired improperly, you may be settling for far less than you should.

If your employment contract called for severance pay to be waived if the employer fired you for good cause, be careful that the employer is not concocting a reason for firing you. The company shouldn't fire you for a minor infraction in your records from years ago, and it shouldn't be doing it for trivial offences such as revealing non-sensitive corporate information in a job application to new employer.

Finally, be aware that if the employer offers you a severance package and you turn it down, the employer is no longer obligated to offer you that package (although many will do so out of a sense of fair play).

Quitting a Job to Job Hunt Full-Time

If you're bored on your present job and feel that it's time to make a change, you may think that it's better to quit first so that you can devote full time to job hunting rather than sending out resumes while you're still working. Don't quit! It's a lot easier to get another job while you're still working, and it's definitely easier to negotiate a good deal when you have to quit your present job to start the new one.

Before you give up on your current job, though, consider the possibility that you're going through job burnout. Is it really necessary to make this drastic move, or could you revive your interest in your present employer? Here are some of the things that cause job burnout and a few solutions:

- ▷ You've lost your mentor. Work used to be exciting because you had a boss who believed in you and encouraged you. That mentor got promoted and your new boss doesn't take the same interest in you. Solution: Work out a career plan with your new boss. Find out what you'd have to do to get the next promotion and work out a plan. Sell yourself to your current boss the way you would to a new employer.
- ▷ Your company has downsized, and fewer and fewer people are doing more and more work. It has become a grind. Solution: Research solutions to the dilemma by researching ways to mechanize the work. Would new software speed things up? Can the department be reorganized to be more efficient? Are some tasks obsolete and you're only doing them because you've always done them that way? Be the hero who creates the solutions.
- ▷ You've been doing the same job for so long now that your work no longer challenges you. You'll never make the big bucks being a drone. As I point out in my real estate investing book *The Weekend Millionaire's Secrets to Investing in Real Estate* (written with Mike Summey; McGraw-Hill) real estate investors have a saying: "Changing use changes value." That means that real estate will always go up in value because of scarcity or inflation, but will take a dramatic jump in value if you change its use. If you buy a home on a main street

and get it zoned commercial so that it can be used for a business, the property takes a big jump in value. If you buy an apartment building and convert it into condos so that you can sell them separately, the building takes a big jump in value. That principle applies to people, too. You'll get cost-of-living increase if you stay doing the same work you're doing now, but if you want to take a dramatic jump in income you've got to change your use to the company. Solution: Take some courses at a local college. Take a look at the audio and video courses offered by my audio publisher, the Nightingale Conant Company (*www.nightingale.com*). Attend your industry conventions so that you can learn about new trends. Then learn some specific skills that can lead to a more exciting and lucrative future.

Leaving With Dignity

So you've landed a new job that pays much better than your current job, which makes you feel that your current employer has cheated you. Should you let the old employer know how you feel because it would help the employer in the future?

Absolutely not! There is a protocol about leaving an employer that says you never criticize the old company, you never talk about the new company, and you do everything you can to leave on good terms. Remember that you will probably need a good reference from this employer.

Make your resignation letter short and to the point:

"I have accepted a position with another company and will leave your employ at the end of the month, unless you want me to leave sooner. I have enjoyed my time here and have nothing but respect and admiration for the company, the management, and the other employees."

No doubt your fellow employees will try to find out where you're going and why you're leaving, but don't tell them. "I'm not telling anyone where I'm going because I don't want to imply that the grass is any greener there. I hope that we'll remain friends after I leave and you'll hear all about it then."

That's class, and it's the way to go out. Then you'll be able to look back on your time at this company with pride.

Key Points to Consider:

- Don't give up on getting severance pay because you were fired from your last job. State law may require it, and the employer may be willing to pay to make your departure a smooth one.
- Don't let your employer build up a trivial offense as a reason to fire you.
- Don't quit your present job to look for something better.
- The grass may look greener on the other side of the fence, but it still needs cutting. Do everything you can to resolve the problems with your present employer before you decide to jump ship.
- Leave your present job with dignity. "Take this job and shove it" is a country western song, not a career-building strategy.

Chapter 10 ▸▸▸

Getting a Raise in Your Present Job

You're doing a good job and you want your present boss to increase your pay. What should you do?

Other than token cost-of-living increases, it's hard to get bosses to dig into their pockets and pay you more of their profits. If you want to substantially improve your income, it will be a lot easier if you get yourself promoted within the company. You should have a plan to achieve the position you want at the company and share that plan with your boss. Let's say that you're a salesperson:

- ▷ Within 18 months you want to be promoted to a district sales manager.
- ▷ In two more years you want to be regional sales manager.
- ▷ Within two more years you want to be national sales manager.
- ▷ In two more years you want to be VP of marketing.

Talk this over with the president of your company and see if it's realistic. Ask what you would have to accomplish in each position to be worthy of the next step. Your president will love you for this. He's got a highly motivated and ambitious employee who wants to do a great job at each stage. You've got a workable plan for increased income and you won't have to grovel for cost-of-living increases.

Key Points to Consider:

- To get more money in your present job, develop a career plan and coordinate it with your boss.
- You will never get rich on cost-of-living increases. You must increase your value to your employer if you expect meaningful earnings increases.

Part Four

Closing Tactics

If you're a salesperson, you're probably very familiar with closing tactics. If you're not in sales, this may be all new to you. A closing tactic is a technique to get the other person to agree to something faster than he or she otherwise would.

When do you use closing tactics in salary negotiations? In four places:

- ▷ A personnel assistant has called you to discuss your resume and get more details from you. Closing tactics will help you convert this to a face-to-face interview.
- ▷ You are having a preliminary interview at the company. Closing tactics will help you get to the next round of interviews.
- ▷ You've had several interviews but the company is not yet ready to make an offer. Closing tactics will help you get an offer on the table.
- ▷ You have countered a salary offer. Closing tactics will help you get a positive response faster.

If you're applying for a sales or sales management job, closing tactics serve another purpose. They let you demonstrate your selling skills to the prospective employer. If the company is hiring a salesperson, the employer expects you to sell him or her on hiring you. If you don't sell yourself hard and well, he or she will be disappointed!

In this section, I'm going to teach you some of the closing tactics that I've seen top salespeople use to get the sale, when a lesser salesperson would have settled for a "let me think it over." I first made my living selling when I was 18 years old, and I've been selling or managing salespeople ever since. In that time I've seen these closes work miracles, and if you memorize them by reading this section over and over, they'll do wonders for your salary negotiations.

Chapter 11 ▸▸▸ The Tugboat Close

If you've ever stood on the banks of the mighty Mississippi, you've no doubt marveled at the tugboats that haul the barges down the river. A tiny tugboat no more than 30 feet long can pull a string of barges, each one weighed down with more than 10,000 tons of cargo. When I sail my sailboat near Los Angeles harbor I watch with amazement as a tiny tugboat can maneuver a 300,000-ton super-tanker. What's the secret of the tugboat's incredible power? The tugboat skipper knows that he can move the largest load if he does it a little bit at a time. If he tried to force that super-tanker to change its direction, he couldn't do it. However hard he revved up his engines and attacked that super-tanker, he would only bounce off. A little bit at a time he can do the most incredible things.

What does this have to do with negotiating a salary? A little bit at a time, you can do the most amazing things. A little bit at a time, you can move the most intractable HR director around and get him or her to make you an offer.

I once got a $250,000 loan from a banker using the Tugboat Close. I owned 33 houses with another investor and I wanted to buy him out so that I would own them all. To do it we needed to get this banker to make a $250,000 loan secured only by a second mortgage on the property. At first, the bank refused to make such a risky investment. The other investor and I asked to meet with the vice president, who only restated his position. However, we gently persisted, knowing that as long as he wouldn't throw us out, we were getting closer to getting the loan approved. An hour later he had agreed to make the loan if we would cross secure it with a $100,000 certificate of deposit. We continued to restate our position without any confrontation, knowing that we were nudging him around. Another hour later he agreed to make the loan secured only by the property.

The next time you're in an employment interview where you're convinced that the employer will never change his mind about making you an offer, think of those tugboats nudging that huge oil tanker around. Employers do change their minds. Just because they told you "no" a minute ago, an hour ago, or yesterday, doesn't necessarily mean that they'll say no again if you ask them one more time. A little bit at a time, you can change anyone's mind.

Chapter 12 ▸▸▸
The Paddock Close

When I was a teenager, I attended the London School of Photography for two years. During my vacations, I earned extra money by photographing thoroughbred horses for breeders. This is a unique branch of photography because the breeders don't want any photographic style. They need a photograph that looks like any other photograph of a horse at stud, so that the breeders can accurately evaluate it. It's a side shot with the far legs of the horse slightly advanced so that the breeders can see all four legs.

It's difficult to get temperamental thoroughbred stallions to stand that way. If you lead the horse in front of the camera and he's not standing properly, you can tug on his leg all you want, but he'll just put it back the way he decided to stand in the first place. That's the way some applicants try to change the employer's mind—with brute force.

The only way to change the way the stallion was standing was to get his mind off the way he decided to stand before. I would lead him around the paddock, talking gently to him to get his mind off the decision he had made earlier. Then I would lead him back in front of the camera and see how he was standing now. If he still wasn't standing the way I wanted him to, I would patiently lead him around the paddock once more and try again.

Some employers can be likened to those stallions. They say no to you for no better reason than because that horse decided to stand with its legs together. When that happens, remember the stallion, and take them for a mental walk around the paddock. Don't try to force them to change their minds. Instead, tell a little story to take their mind off the decision they made. Think to yourself, "I asked the right closing question but my timing was off. I'll distract them and return to the closing question in a few minutes." After you've mentally walked them around the paddock, go for the close again. If they still say no, walk them around the paddock again, and, after you've distracted them with a story, go for the close again.

Great salespeople can do that five or six times without becoming frustrated. Excellent salespeople can do it 10 or 12 times and persist. Never think of a no as a refusal—simply think of it as a sign that you need to walk the HR director around the paddock one more time.

Chapter 13 ▸▸▸

The "That Wouldn't Stop You" Close

This is the simplest close that I'm going to teach you, and it will probably seem ludicrous to you. But until you've tried it, you won't believe how powerful it can be.

My son Dwight taught it to me when he was selling new cars. Whenever he had a customer raise an objection, instead of trying to argue that the customer was wrong or find a way to work around the objection, he learned to say, "But that wouldn't stop you from going ahead today, would it?" At first, he felt stupid doing it because he was sure that the customer would ridicule him. However, he discovered that a remarkable number of times the buyers would back away from the objection. They would say, "You only have the car in red? We wanted green."

He would respond, "But that wouldn't stop you from going ahead today, would it?"

And they would say, "Well no, I guess it wouldn't."

It sounds outrageous, doesn't it? But if you try it, I think you will end up kicking yourself, because you'll find that objections that you would think would be deal killers don't need a response. The employer says, "You don't have any experience in making left-handed widgets."

You say, "But that wouldn't stop you from hiring me and training me, would it?"

He may well say, "Well I guess not, if you're willing to work as hard as you say you will."

The mark of a Power Closer is that he or she knows that he or she doesn't have to satisfy every objection. If you decide to counter every objection the employer brings up, you'll begin to feel that you're in a shooting gallery where, every time you knock down one objection, another one pops up.

Chapter 14 ▸▸▸

The "You Can Afford It" Close

My travel agent used this close on me to get me to spend $7,000 that I had no intention of spending. With the right person in the right circumstances, I think that it's very powerful.

Several years ago, my daughter Julia and I decided to spend a month in Africa. The trip would include a climb of Mount Kilimanjaro in Tanzania and a visit to a game preserve in Kenya. Just before we left, we happened to see the movie *Gorillas in the Mist*, the story of Diane Fosse's fight to save the almost-extinct mountain gorillas in Rwanda. Fascinated by this I called my travel agent, Tess Vizon, to see if we could visit the gorillas while we were in Africa. She started checking and called me back a few days later. "There are only 29 silverback gorillas left in the world," she told me. "They are all in the area in Central Africa where Rwanda, Uganda, and Zaire meet. Because there are so few and none of them are in captivity, it's almost impossible to visit them. However, the brother of the president of Zaire owns a small lodge up in mountains and I can get you in the week before Christmas. It will cost you an extra $7,000 dollars to do it."

When I heard the price, I almost choked. We were not naturalists with a lifetime ambition to see these gorillas. All we'd done was go see a movie and become curious about them. "Tess," I said, "I'm not sure I want to pay $7,000 to see some gorillas."

Her response was brilliant. She said, "Oh, come on Roger. You want to do it. You can afford to do it. Go ahead and do it."

I thought that it was one of the best closes I'd ever heard. Of course she flattered me by thinking that I had that much money to throw around, but the truth was that I *could* afford to do it and I *did* want to do it. I told her to book it, and it turned out to be the highlight of our trip.

Remember the "You Can Afford It Close" when you're dealing with an employer who is choking on how much money you're asking him or her to pay you. He's saying, "I've never paid $200,000 for a sales manager in my life!" You smile and say, "Come on! You know I'll do a terrific job for you, and you can afford me. Go ahead and hire me!" Remember that you've got to build the desire to hire you first. It's not going to work unless he or she is drooling to get you on board.

Chapter 15 ▶▶▶

The "Leave 'Em Alone" Close

When I was a teenager in England, I sold appliances for a living, and I frequently sold to husbands and wives. I learned that I could really raise my closing percentages if I left them alone for a few minutes toward the end of my presentation. If I stayed with them the whole time, I risked losing the sale. You see, however well they knew each other, they couldn't read the other person's mind. They weren't sure if their spouse wanted to buy or not. Leaving them alone for a while gives them a chance to ask each other, "What do you think, dear?"

This doesn't just apply to husbands and wives. You might be selling yourself to the president and vice president of a company. The president may be eager to go ahead and hire you, but he or she wants to be sure that the vice president is "on board" and will enthusiastically support the hire. Or the vice president may be eager, but isn't sure if the president will overrule him or her. Give them some time alone to resolve those issues, and getting hired will be easier for you.

Once I learned the art of leaving them alone for a while, much of my problem in closing sales went away.

Don't make the employers ask you for time to talk it over; give it to them. You don't have to say, "Let me give you time to think about it." Simply find an excuse to leave them for a few minutes, such as fetching coffee or using the restroom.

Chapter 16 ▸▸▸
The Vince Lombardi Close

This is a terrific close for add-on items such as a company car or country club membership. When you're selling yourself to a prospective employer, a psychological resistance sometimes builds up in his or her mind. As employers approach the point of making a decision, they start to resist making the decision. Perhaps they feel anxious that they may be doing the wrong thing, or that they're not getting the best deal from you. Whatever the reason, the tension builds until the moment they make the decision to hire you. Then, once the decision has been made to hire you, a remarkable change takes place in their mind. Having made the decision, their mind does anything it can to reinforce the decision they just made. That's when you can get them to give you a company car or a corner office.

Car salespeople know this, don't they? They know that if they can close you on any make and model of car, even a stripped-down one, then they can get you into the closing room and add on all the other little extras that really build the profit into the car.

One rule of Power Closing is that you don't have to close on everything up front. Once you reach that point of agreement, the employer stops being your opponent and becomes your partner in business success. That's when you can make the second effort and add on all of those valuable extras.

Vince Lombardi always used to talk about the second effort. He loved to show his Green Bay Packers film clips of receivers who almost caught the ball but couldn't quite hang on to it. But instead of letting it go, they made a second effort and caught it before it hit the ground. Or running backs who were tackled but still managed to wriggle free and make the touchdown. Vince Lombardi would tell his players that everybody is out there making the first effort. They wouldn't be on the team if they didn't know how to play the game well and were out there doing everything that he told them to do. But everybody's doing that. Every team in the league is doing that. The difference, Vince Lombardi would say, between the good players and the great players is that the great players will make that second effort. When everyone else thinks that the play is lost, they'll still keep trying.

Perhaps you're having your first interview with the company and you sense that it's not going well. They're beginning to conclude the interview without any talk of a second interview. You might say, "I'm sure that you have tests that you like to give applicants. Why don't I take those tests as long as I'm here?" Making that second effort will keep you in the group of people who are still being considered.

The difference between negotiating a good salary offer and a great employment package often rests with your ability to make that extra effort. When every other applicant would be saying, "This is a good job offer. Don't push your luck," you make one more effort. If you want to be a great closer, take a tip from Vince Lombardi: When everyone else is saying, "Give up. You've tried hard enough," you need to give it one more effort.

Chapter 17 ▶▶▶

The Silent Close

The Silent Close is always a fun one to use. It goes like this: Make your salary request and then **shut up!** From then on, the first person who talks, loses.

Employers can respond to your salary request in one of three ways: They can say yes, they can say no, or they can let you know that they can't decide. If you're a positive thinker, you expect them to say yes. You will be surprised if they say no, or that they can't decide. Wait to find out. Until you find out that they won't say yes, don't change your proposal.

I once made an offer on a building to a seller who was asking $240,000. My offer was $180,000. Frankly, it scared me half to death to present an offer that low. I thought the seller would be furious that I wasted his time. I gritted my teeth and read the offer to him. Then I turned the offer around, pushed it across the desk, and laid my pen on top of it for him to sign.

He looked at it for a while, and then he picked it up and read it all way through, including the fine print. He laid it down and looked at me. I bit my tongue to stop myself from talking.

He picked the offer up again and read it all the way through one more time. Then he put it down and looked at me again, for what seemed to be five minutes.

Finally he said, "I suppose that now I'm supposed to say yes, no, or maybe. Is that right?"

I smiled slightly but still didn't say anything. He picked it up for the third time and read it all the way through. Then he said, "I'll tell you what I'll do. I won't accept this, but I will accept this." He wrote a very acceptable counter-proposal on the bottom of the offer, turned it around, and slid it back across the desk to me.

The Silent Close is the simplest to understand and one of the hardest to use. We're not used to silence. Even a minute of silence seems to be an eternity.

Remember: Always assume the employer will say yes to your salary request. Don't say a word until you find out whether he or she will accept your request, or whether he or she won't.

Chapter 18 ▸▸▸

The "Subject To" Close

The "Subject To" Close is a great way to handle the employer who is intimidated by the size of the decision that you're asking him or her to make. In real estate, we understood that when our customers were buying a new home, it was probably the largest investment they would ever make. We knew that we had found the perfect home for them, but sometimes the enormity of the decision would stop them from going ahead. I would teach our agents to say, "Why don't we just write it up subject to you being approved for the financing?" By making the sale conditional on another event taking place, you appear to be turning a major decision into a minor one. Naturally, a good real estate agent knows that you will qualify for the financing, so you really just purchased a home.

The life insurance agent realizes that his buyer is having trouble agreeing to his proposal. He says, "Frankly, I don't know if I can get this much insurance on someone of your age. It would be subject to your passing the physical, so why don't we just write up the paperwork subject to your passing the physical." It doesn't sound as though you've made as big a decision as you really have. However, the agent knows that if his customer can fog a mirror during that physical, he can find someone, somewhere, who will underwrite that policy.

When you sense some resistance from the employer to making a decision, try the "Subject To" Close. You might say, "Obviously, you'll want me to pass an editing test before you make a final decision. Why don't we agree that you'll hire me subject to me passing the test?" It doesn't sound to the employer as if he or she is making as big a decision as he really is. In reality, of course, you know that you can ace that editing test.

Chapter 19 ▸▸▸

The Ben Franklin Close

If you're a salesperson, I'm sure that you've heard of the Ben Franklin Close before. It's based on something Franklin wrote to the British chemist Joseph Priestley about the way he made decisions. He wrote:

> *My way (of making decisions) is to divide a sheet of paper into two columns; writing over the one Pro, and over the other Con. Then, during the three or four days consideration, I put down under the different heads short hints of the different motives, that at different times occur to me, for or against the measure. When I have thus got them all together in one view, I endeavor to estimate their respective weights; and where I find two, on each side, that seem equal, I strike them both out. If I find a reason pro equal to some two reasons con, I strike out all three. If I judge some two reasons con, equal to some three reasons pro, I strike out the five; and thus proceeding I find at length where the balance lies; and if, after a day or two of further considerations, nothing new that is of importance occurs on either side, I come to a determination accordingly.*

The Ben Franklin Close is designed to make people feel better when they have trouble making up their mind. When using this as a closing technique there is an essential preamble. Unless you use the preamble, the Ben Franklin close won't work. Before you use the close you say, "Mr. Employer, I'm not surprised that you're having trouble making a decision, because many intelligent people do. For example, one of our greatest statesmen, Ben Franklin, had trouble making decisions. Let me tell you what he used to do. See if you think it's a good way for you to make up your mind. When Ben couldn't make up his mind he would simply take a sheet of paper and draw a line down the middle. On the left-hand side he'd list all the reasons for going ahead with the project and on the right hand side, he would list all the reason for not going ahead with the project. If the reasons for going ahead exceeded the reasons for not going ahead, he would decide to proceed. Doesn't that make sense for you, too?" It's important to get the employer's agreement that he or she will go along with this method before you go ahead with the analysis. If you don't, you can go through the entire exercise and still have him or her telling you that he or she wants to think it over.

Having gotten the employer's agreement that it's a good way to decide, start listing the reasons for his hiring you. On this side of the list, give him all the help you can. "You like the fact that I'm familiar with your product? You do agree that a business finance degree is a big plus?" Help him make that left-hand column as long as it can be. However, when you exhaust the reasons for going ahead and hiring you, and start on the reasons for not going ahead, he's on his own. Doing it this way, your list of positives has to exceed the list of negatives and you'll get the employer's agreement.

Chapter 20 ▸▸▸
The Dumb Mistake Close

Sometimes you'd like to climb over the desk and tell the employer what a dumb mistake he or she is making by being reluctant to hire you. You can't do this, of course, because it would antagonize the employer. The Dumb Mistake Close is a way of telling her what a dumb mistake she's making without actually accusing her of it. The difference is that you tell her a story about someone else who made a dumb mistake when she was in the same situation.

When I ran a real estate company, we would often have buyers who balked when they saw the amount of the monthly payment on the loan. I would teach the agents to tell this story:

"You know what I wish? I wish the president of our company, Roger Dawson, were here. He tells the story about the first house he ever bought. He went down to the bank to sign the loan papers and realized that he would be committing to pay $67 a month for 30 years. He started to figure that out what a huge commitment that was and got cold feet. Fortunately, the loan officer realized the problem, took pity on him, and broke the rules by saying, "You have to go ahead. The papers are all prepared." He obediently went ahead and signed the papers. Within a few years the house doubled in value. If Roger were here now, he'd tell you to close your eyes and sign. It seems like a great deal of money now, but five years from now it won't. You'll look at it as the smartest move you ever made."

I remember buying a bicycle for my son John when he was young. This was before helmets became mandatory for cyclists in California. After we'd picked out the bike the storeowner selected an expensive helmet and said, "You'll need this, too." Of course, my son's safety concerned me, but I had ridden a bike throughout my childhood and I never had a helmet but survived just fine, so it seemed to be an unnecessary expense. The storeowner said, "Oh I wish Mr. Jones was here now. He lives up on Skyline Drive and last month he bought a bike for his son Bobby. He didn't want to invest in a helmet either. The next day he was riding down Church Hill Drive and went straight into a car coming up the hill. He was seriously injured and for the rest of my life, I'll have to live with the knowledge that I didn't insist on him getting a helmet. I wish Mr. Jones were here now, because he'd tell you how important it is." Guess who grabbed that helmet out of her hands and rammed it onto his son's head?

The Dumb Mistake Close is a terrific way to put pressure on the employer without confrontation. You're applying for a job that involves you relocating and the employer is reluctant to pay your moving expenses. "I understand exactly how you feel about that," you say. "It is a big investment and you're probably concerned that I wouldn't stay. Let me reassure you. If I don't stay for a year, I'll repay you every penny and I'll put that in writing. But don't let it stop you from hiring me if you think I'm the right person for the job. I remember at my previous company our sales manager was faced with a similar dilemma. He didn't hire a salesperson with top potential because he was concerned about the moving expenses. I wish he was here now, because he would tell you it was the biggest mistake he ever made."

Chapter 21 ▸▸▸

The Final Objection Close

Sometimes when I'm training salespeople, I'll ask an audience member in the front row to stand up and lock hands with me. Then I start to push against his or her hands. Invariably he or she pushes back. People are that way: If you push them too hard they'll nearly always push back. The Final Objection Close removes the pressure of closing the sale and stops them from pushing against you.

To make it work you have to appear defeated, as though you've given up trying to sell them on hiring you. "Okay," you say. "I accept that you're not going to hire me, but just to clarify my thinking would you mind telling me why you decided not to go ahead? What did I do wrong?"

"You didn't do anything wrong," the employer might tell you. "You interviewed well."

"Then it must be my reference or lack of experience."

"No, that's not it either. It's just that you're asking for more than we can pay you."

"Well that makes me feel better," you say. "I'm glad it wasn't anything I did to offend you. The only reason you're not going ahead is the salary?"

Once you've narrowed it down to the Final Objection by removing the appearance of still trying to close, you have only to answer that objection to make the sale. For this close to work you must go through these four stages:

1. Appear defeated.
2. Release the pressure.
3. Get the HR director to narrow it down to one objection.
4. Overcome that objection.

Perhaps you overcome the objection by making a small concession. "Let me suggest this compromise. I'll come on board for $5,000 less than I suggested if you'd agree to take another look at my salary in 90 days. Fair enough?"

Chapter 22 ▸▸▸

The Puppy Dog Close

I'm sure that you've heard the story of the petstore owner who's trying to sell the little boy a puppy. When the boy says he can't decide, the owner suggests that he take the puppy home for the weekend, telling him, "If you don't like him you can bring him back on Monday." He's sure that by Monday the little boy will have fallen in love with the puppy and won't dream of bringing him back.

Back in the 1950s, my first sales job was in an appliance store where we sold thousands of televisions using the Puppy Dog Close. In those days, television was new to most people, and you might be the only person on your street to have one. Your neighbors even expected you to invite them over to watch it, and serve them tea and sandwiches. If we had a potential customer who couldn't decide, we would suggest that we would put it into their home for a trial. We knew the minute the neighbors saw the antenna being erected on the roof they would be asking if they could come over to watch television. How could they not keep the television after the neighbors had been over to spend the evening watching it?

At the real estate company I ran, I would encourage the sales associates to carry an instant camera with them. When a buyer made an offer on a new home, we would take a picture of them in front of the house knowing that they would show the picture to their friends and relatives. Then if the owner wouldn't accept the buyer's offer, we knew that the buyer was much more likely to raise the offer. Who wants to tell their friends that they couldn't afford to pay more?

The Puppy Dog Close is harder to use in employment negotiations because it involves being willing to work without pay for a while, but it could be appropriate. My good friend Syd Bezonsky told me about moving from Montreal to Los Angeles when he was a young man. It was in the middle of a severe recession and he couldn't find any work in his trade, which was as a printer. The printers union had 70 skilled printers who couldn't find work. Syd found a non-union printer and told him, "I need to work. Let me come to work for you for no pay. If you like what I do, you can pay me, but you don't have to." The printer was so impressed with Syd's willingness to work that he gave him a chance. Soon Syd had doubled his machines' capacity and the printer was happy to pay even more than union scale.

If nothing else works, try the Puppy Dog Close and suggest, "Let me come to work for you for a week without pay. I won't charge you a dime. Give me a chance to show you what I can do; that's all I'm asking for."

The truth of the matter is that very few employers will take you up on that offer, but it will convince them that you are sincere and eager to work.

Chapter 23 ▸▸▸

The Minor Point Close

When you're selling yourself to an employer, little decisions lead up to big decisions. If you can get your customer to agree on minor points, you are clarifying his or her thinking so that when you get ready for the major decision he or she is less likely to feel pressured.

The car salesperson asks the buyer:

- ▷ "If you did go ahead, would you want leather or vinyl upholstery?"
- ▷ "Would you want the stick shift or the automatic?"
- ▷ "Would you prefer white or red?"

The real estate salesperson asks:

- ▷ "If you chose this home, which of these bedrooms would be the nursery for your new baby?"
- ▷ "How would you arrange the furniture in the living room?"

In salary negotiations you ask:

- ▷ "If we did agree on this, would I be able to give my employer two weeks' notice?"
- ▷ "Would I immediately get the employee discount?"
- ▷ "How would you make the announcement about me coming on board with you?"
- ▷ "If you agreed to pay my moving expenses, would you pay the mover directly or would you reimburse me?"

Chapter 24 ▸▸▸

The Positive Assumption Close

This may seem obvious to you, but it's essential to assume that the employer is going to want to hire you. It amazes me how many people make a negative assumption—they seem surprised if the employer makes an offer! If you walked into a restaurant and the server came up and asked you if you *wanted* to order food, she would confuse you, wouldn't she? She knows what you're there for and simply assumes that you're going to buy food. You should do the same thing with your job interviews. Always assume that they're going to want you and make you a good offer.

I believe that fear of the employer not wanting you is at the heart of high-pressure selling, and it's why employers hate it when you try to pressure them into hiring you. There's no need to pressure a customer when you assume that he or she will buy. High-pressure tactics come only from applicants who fear that the employer is not going to want them.

Keep your conversation positive. Say, "I think that we're a good match, don't you?" not "Do you think I'm right for this job?"

Always make positive assumptions—that they're going to want you, that they're going to make you an offer, that they're going to do it today, and that everything is going to go through without a hitch.

Chapter 25 ▸▸▸

The Return Serve Close

This close teaches you that when the buyer asks you a question, you should usually reply with a question. Many years ago, I was buying a used copy machine from an attorney. I asked, "Would you take $200 for it?" He said, "Are you offering me $200?" I thought, "How smart." If he'd have told me instead that he would take $200, I probably would have hummed and hawed around before offering him even less.

When the HR director looks as though he or she is close to making a decision to buy and serve you a clarifying question, return the serve. In doing so, you'll be getting a commitment. When the employer says, "Can you start right away?" say, "Would you like me to start right away?" "Would you work on salary plus commission?" should cause you to respond, "Are you offering me salary plus commission?"

Chapter 26 ▸▸▸

The Alternate Choice Close

When you ask people to choose between one of two alternatives, they will usually pick one of the two. Very seldom will they select the third option, that neither of the two choices is acceptable.

Frankly, whenever I use the Alternate Choice Close, its effectiveness surprises me all over again. Before customers have made a decision to buy I will say, "If you did go ahead, would you use your American Express Card or your MasterCard?" They nearly always pick one of the two. Then I say, "Would you like me to fill out the form for you, or would you rather do it yourself?" With just a couple of quick alternate choice questions, I have closed the sale. The interesting thing is that even if they know what you're doing, people seem irresistibly drawn to picking one of the two alternatives.

Be sure that both of the options are acceptable to you. "Do you want it or not?" is not a smart alternate choice!

This is such a well-known close that you'll even hear little children using it. "Dad, would you like to take me to the video arcade tonight, or would tomorrow night be better for you?" As a grandson goes into the ice cream store he says, "Grandpa, are we going to get doubles or triples today?"

You can also use the Alternate Choice Close for setting appointments. Assume that when the personnel assistant calls, he or she wants to meet with you and ask, "Would Monday or Tuesday be better for you?" or "Would 10 o'clock or 11 be better for you?"

Salespeople know that you must narrow the choices down to two. It won't work with three options, so they need to eliminate the third option. If they sell cars they might say, "I think the first one we looked at would be too small for you, so it's between the red one and the white one. Which did you prefer?" If they sell real estate and they've shown the buyer three properties they might say, "I got the feeling that you didn't like the master bedroom in the first house, so if you were going to go ahead with one of the other two, which one would it be?"

Use the Alternate Choice Close every chance you get. You might say, "Of the two openings that you have, which do you think I'd be better suited for?"

Chapter 27 ▶▶▶
The Doorknob Close

As with the Final Objection Close, the Doorknob Close is dependent upon you being able to release the employer from the pressure of the buying decision.

When you have tried everything else and still don't have an offer from the employer, close your briefcase and say, "It was really nice talking with you, even though you decided not to make me an offer. I can understand your feelings about that. Perhaps sometime in the future we can get together again." You appear to be leaving, but as your hand hits the doorknob on the way out of his or her office, you pause pensively and say, "Would you mind helping me? I always try to learn something from every employment interview. Would you mind telling me what I did wrong? It will help me so much in the future."

As long as he feels that you're no longer trying to sell him, he'll often be helpful enough to share with you why he didn't make you an offer. He may say, "You came on too strong, too early. We felt pressured." Or he may say, "We liked what you were showing us but we just can't afford to pay you what you were making on your last job, and we didn't want to insult you with a lower offer."

Now you can move to the Vince Lombardi Second Effort Close. Gently thank him for sharing and slide back into your presentation. Remember that the Doorknob Close will only work if you're able to convince him or her that you're no longer trying to sell him or her on hiring you. You're only asking for help on how to improve your interviewing skills.

Chapter 28 ▸▸▸ The Divide and Conquer Close

You may have to use the Divide and Conquer Close any time that you are trying to sell to two people. I've noticed that opposites attract when it comes to assertiveness levels. A less assertive person will often marry a more assertive person. A businessperson who has a warm and easygoing personality—a people person—will often have a much more assertive business partner. They make a good team. The assertive no-nonsense person admires the warm human qualities of the less assertive person. The easygoing people person admires the discipline and firmness of the more assertive person.

An assertive person is a fast decision-maker. He or she will look at your application and consider how your interview went and make you an offer quickly. A less assertive person agonizes over decisions, and that analysis frequently leads to paralysis.

When you're faced with this, you should use the Divide and Conquer close. Get the more assertive person aside and say, "Mr. Jones, I really admire the analysis that your HR director Roy is doing here. But what concerns me, Mr. Jones, is that we're never going to get together if you don't decide soon. You know that I'm right for this job, don't you?" He might go to the HR director and say, "Roy, knock it off, for heaven's sake. This is the right person for the job and we should get her on board right away." Chances are that Roy will say, "If that's what you want to do, it's fine with me."

Similarly, with business partners, you may have to find a way to get the more assertive person aside and say, "I get the feeling that you're the decision-maker around here, Bob. You know that I can do a terrific job for you. Let's move on it before it's too late." Chances are he'll say something such as, "Don't worry about it. You have a deal. I just have to be diplomatic about the way I handle it with Harry."

Whenever you're selling yourself to two people and one of them is more assertive than the other, use the Divide and Conquer Close. Find a way to separate them and get the decision from the more assertive partner.

Chapter 29 ▸▸▸

The Let 'Em Think Close

With some people, it's easy to tell when they're thinking. They use a pad of paper and fill it with numbers and options, or they pull out a calculator and punch in numbers furiously. With others, it's harder to tell when they're thinking because they just go quiet and work out the decision in their mind. That's a particular problem for salespeople, because salespeople can't stand silence. They think it means that the customer has lost interest and needs you to stimulate him or her with conversation. But sometimes you just have to give them time to think.

I remember when I was investing heavily in income-producing real estate. Many times an agent would take me out to show me an apartment building that he or she wanted to sell me. In the car on the way back, I would need time to think it through. How much would it cost me to improve the property? How high could I raise the rents? Where would I generate the cash for the down payment? How would I handle the management? I prefer to do all this in my mind and verify my calculations later. To the agent it must have looked as though I was totally disinterested. All too often, the agent would interpret this as meaning that he or she had to give me more information to stimulate my interest. Nothing could be further from the truth. I simply needed some quiet time to think about it.

If the employer seems to be deep in thought, assume that he or she is trying to figure out how much to offer you and be quiet while they think it through.

Chapter 30 ▸▸▸ The Bank Note Close

If you enjoy theatrics, you'll get a kick out of the drama of the Bank Note Close. You use it when employers don't want to hire you because they feel they can find someone better.

Take a $20 bill out of your pocket, drop it on the floor, and put your toe on it. Then say, "Let me ask you this. If you were walking along the sidewalk and saw a $20 bill lying there, would you pick it up? Of course you would. It's an opportunity that exists for you, just as the opportunity to put me to work for you is an opportunity. You wouldn't pass up the opportunity to pick up the $20 bill because there may be a $50 bill lying further down the sidewalk, would you? But that's exactly what you're doing if you pass up an opportunity as good as the one I showed you today!"

The Bank Note Close is a whimsical one, and you can fault the logic, but the gutsiness of the bank note on the floor may just impress the employer enough to give him or her the impetus to hire you.

Chapter 31 ▸▸▸

The Recall Close

I learned this close as a teenager, when I was selling televisions in England. I learned it by instinct, because we didn't have much sales training in those days. I quickly figured out that it wasn't good to tell the customer everything you knew about the product. It was smart to leave something out that you could suddenly recall in case you're not able to close them.

Perhaps I would demonstrate a television to them and they would show interest in it, but tell me that they wanted to look in some other stores before they made up their mind. I would wish them the best of luck and then, just as they approached the door on the way out of the showroom, I would call out, "Just a minute folks. I just recalled that I didn't show you something very important about this television. Did you know that the wood finish on the cabinet is completely resistant to cigarette burns? You can grind out a cigarette on it and it won't damage it. Let me show you." Then I would lead them back to the television, demonstrate the feature, get back into my sales presentation, and go for the close again.

Whenever I think of this, I remember the manufacturer's representative who first told us about this new miracle finish. All the salespeople in the showroom gathered around to watch his demonstration. He lit up a cigarette and with a great flourish ground it out on the wood top of the set. He was waiting for our eyes to light up in amazement, so he was watching us. We were watching the cigarette as it slowly melted the finish on the top of the set. With growing horror, he suddenly realized that he was demonstrating on one of the older models that didn't yet have the burn-resistant finish! I'm sure that even today, 40 years later, he still blushes when he thinks about that day.

A car salesperson might deliberately not tell a prospect about the special lock that enables the driver to unlock the driver's door without unlocking the passenger door. Then the salesperson can call the prospect up and say, "I can't believe this but I just recalled that I didn't tell you something very important. I'd like to bring the car by this evening and show it to you. Would seven or eight o'clock be better for you?" You've heard of buyer's remorse, of course, but non-buyer's remorse is a reality, too. The customer may be sitting there thinking, "I wish I'd brought that car home with me today." She still wants to be sold because she feels guilty spending that much money, so she may not be willing to call the salesman. However, she'll welcome it when the salesman calls and gives her a second chance to invest.

Whatever you present yourself to an employer, don't tell him or her all the benefits of having you on the payroll. Always leave something out for the Recall Close. You might call and say, "I can't believe that I didn't tell you about this today, but I'm a certified Webpage designer. If you ever needed help with that I could do it for you. Could I stop by tomorrow and show you some of my work?"

Chapter 32 ▸▸▸

The Take Control Close

Some HR people have a terrible time making a decision. They tend to be so touchy-feely that they don't want to offend anyone. I call them Amiables, the unassertive emotionals of the world. Extreme Amiables find making a decision so traumatic that they won't make a move until someone tells them to. In transactional analysis terms, these people are the "child" personalities. Psychologist Eric Berne took Freud's theory of super ego, id, and ego and simplified it into parent, child, and adult. The superego (or parent part of the personality) restrains the other two parts of the personality. The id (or child part of the personality) tends to act impulsively without thought. The ego (or adult part of the personality) reasons things through.

You would think that the impulsive childlike personality would be the easiest to sell to. After all, their philosophy is: If it feels good, do it. However, over the years this has gotten them into trouble. They may really want to hire you, but they can't decide because they're afraid of the trouble they may get into. In other words, they have cold feet.

These people need to be told to act.

You tell them firmly, "I'm not going to leave here today until you make me an offer. Everything tells me that this is the right decision for you. I'm the perfect match for this job opportunity. I can't leave here today in good conscience without getting your okay, so I'm going to make the decision for you. I know that you think I'm right for the job, so go ahead and say, 'You're hired.'"

Of course, you can only do this if you're convinced that they should. Don't do it just to make a paycheck. However, if you're totally convinced that they'd be making a mistake to say no, this extra push of decisiveness may be the only way you can get them to do the right thing and hire you.

Chapter 33 ▸▸▸

The Dawson Pledge

You might call the Dawson Pledge the last resort. If everything else has failed, I want you to take the Dawson Pledge. You note the time on your watch and you mentally raise your left hand, put your right hand over your heart, and think, "I hereby pledge that I will not leave this employer until another 30 minutes has gone by." Whatever it takes, and even if the HR director never mentions hiring you, stay with it for 30 more minutes.

Ask for another cup of coffee—that'll take five minutes. Pretend it's too hot to drink and you can get 10 minutes out of it. Maybe the pot is empty. That's good. Make them brew another one. Now you're talking half an hour. Whatever it takes, don't leave for 30 more minutes.

Because as all negotiators know, the longer you can keep someone engaged, the more flexible he or she becomes. Just because he or she is telling you no now, doesn't mean that he won't be saying maybe 30 minutes from now and yes an hour from now.

If all else fails, take the Dawson Pledge.

Section II

Negotiating Compensation

Part One

Preparing for the Negotiation

You probably invested in this book for one of three reasons:

- ▷ You'd like to talk your present employer into paying you more.
- ▷ You are up for a promotion and will be negotiating your compensation package.
- ▷ You're applying for a new job and want to cut the best deal you can.

I'm going to teach you a lot of negotiating tactics that will help you negotiate the best deal, but first let's look at the big picture. What makes you valuable to an employer? What positions you to get the best deal?

Chapter 34 ▸▸▸ Power Comes From Having Options

Here's Rule Number One in any negotiation:

Your power is in direct relationship to the options that you have versus the options that the other side has.

At Harvard University they call it BATNA: Best Alternative to a Negotiated Agreement. The side that has the best BATNA has the power in a negotiation. Let's apply that very sound principle to your relationship with an employer.

Your Value Is Directly Related to the Difficulty of Replacing You

I've been applying that rule for most of my life, ever since I started my first business as a resort hotel photographer when I was only 16. I've never come across an exception to the rule. It always applied when I was a personnel director at a large department store and was hiring people every day. It always applied when I was president of a large real estate company in Southern California with 28 offices, 540 sales associates, and a headquarters staff of 50 people. And it still applies today.

Do you ever wonder about the people who collect tolls on bridges and freeways? Don't they realize that on any given day they could show up for work and their cozy little tollbooth would have been torn out and replaced with a mechanical transponder?

What about the people who check you out at the grocery store or the hardware superstore? Don't they understand that they are being replaced every day by self-service checkouts? And that the customers don't miss them?

Check into a big casino hotel in Las Vegas these days. You don't get to talk to a desk clerk. You walk over to a screen and identify yourself by inserting your credit card. The machine assigns you a room and asks you how many keys you want. It instructs you to take blanks out of a box and insert them into the slot to make your key for you. You don't talk to anyone. That's the way it's done in all the mid-level mammoth hotels. It's even an option in the luxury hotels such as the Venetian. And a lot of guests prefer it to lining up to talk to a person.

So how can you use this principle to increase your value to your employer and improve your negotiating situation? Here's the answer:

Do One Part of Your Job so Well That You Become Irreplaceable

You reduce the options that your employer has by doing one part of your job so well that you become irreplaceable. It doesn't have to be everything you do on your job, just one part of it. Do one part so well that they wouldn't know where to find a replacement. For example:

- ▷ Be the physician in the emergency ward who never gets flustered, however great the pressure.
- ▷ Be the police officer who has an uncanny ability to calm down angry people.
- ▷ Be the schoolteacher who can make math sound exciting to even the most reluctant pupil.
- ▷ Be the business manager who has an exceptional ability to spot new trends.

- ▷ Be the receptionist with an amazing ability to handle complaining customers.

When the executive committee meets to discuss your raise or promotion, you want them saying, "He's not perfect in everything he does, but when it comes to _________, there's nobody who can do a better job. I don't know where we'd ever find a replacement."

Remember that your power as a negotiator is in direct relationship to the options that you have versus the options that your boss has. You want to remove the options that your employer has by doing one part of your job so well that you don't think he or she would ever find a replacement.

On the other side of the coin, you want to use this principle to increase your power. How do you increase your power in a salary negotiation? You do it by developing options before you go into the negotiation.

It amazes me how many people will go into a salary negotiation, but they haven't thought through what they are going to do if the boss says no to their request for more money. If only they would think it through a little. If they would say to themselves, "What would I do if I wasn't working here? What options are available to me?"

Even better, make a few phone calls and line up a few options. Then you're started to develop real power.

It doesn't mean that you'll charge into your boss and say, "Give me what I want or I'm out of here!" It does mean that you'll be a more powerful negotiator because you'll be sitting there thinking, "I hope they'll offer me a good deal, but if they don't, I've got these other options that look good to me."

If you want to have ultimate power in a salary negotiation, make the options better than what you're negotiating for. Now you're sitting there thinking, "I'll stay out of a sense of loyalty but I hope that they say no because I really want to go start my own business (or join the Peace Corp, or become a professional golfer).

Your power in a salary negotiation is in direct relationship to the alternatives that you have—versus the alternatives they have. I'm not suggesting that you threaten to quit if you don't get an increase in pay. But to identify which side has the power, you might want to take a piece of paper and draw a line down the middle. On the left hand side of the line, write your alternatives in the event they don't give you what you want. How many other companies are out there that would give you as good an opportunity or better?

On the other side of the line draw a list of their alternatives in the event that you quit over this issue. How easy would it be for them to replace you? In this way you can establish how much power you have in a negotiation.

The third principle that's important here is the principle of being prepared to walk away. It's the number-one pressure point in any negotiation.

A pitcher for the Los Angeles Dodgers was once offered $4 million for a three-year contract. He asked for $8 million and he got $7.9 million. That roughly equates to throwing the ball and sticking $500 in your pocket. Throw it again, and stick another $500 in your pocket. What a country!

How did he get just about everything he wanted? He projected that he was prepared to walk away. Now, he didn't go to the management of the team and say, "Look, if you don't give me what I want I'm out of here." Many people negotiate that way, but it's very confrontational and it creates more problems than are necessary. He was subtle enough to be talking to reporters, saying to them, "Look, don't assume that I'll be back with the Dodgers next year. My contract is up for renewal, and I've had a really good offer from the Japanese. I may go play in Japan for a couple of years." He wasn't going to go play in Japan; he wasn't going to leave the Dodgers, but what a brilliant opening negotiating position! "No problem, I've got all kinds of alternatives."

Don't do this if you're in a weak position with your company. If you are in a strong position, though, it probably would help you to plant a few rumors in the department. Take the biggest gossip in the company to lunch and swear him to secrecy. Lean over and say, "Can I trust you to keep a secret?" The only reason you've sprung for lunch is knowing perfectly well that you can't trust him to keep a secret, but he's going to respond, "Yes, of course you can; you know me." Now he's drooling to hear what you have to say. "Don't mention a word of this, but I may not be here much longer. I've had a terrific offer from a competitor and I'm seriously considering it." If you've picked the right person, the entire office will be talking about it tomorrow, and by the afternoon your boss will be wanting to have a chat with you to assure you of your great future with the company.

So far, I've covered three basic negotiating principles that come into play in this situation:

- ▷ Recognize that your power in the negotiation is your relationship to the alternatives that each side has.
- ▷ Reduce the employer's options by doing one part of your job so well that they wouldn't know where to find a replacement.
- ▷ Realize that the most important pressure point is this: Which side is prepared to walk away from the negotiations if they can't get what they want?

Key Points to Consider:

- Your power in a negotiation comes from convincing the employer that you have options.
- Your value to your employer is directly related to the difficulty of replacing you.
- Do one part of your job so well that you become irreplaceable.

Chapter 35 ▸▸▸

The Magic of the Trade-Off

If you want to justify your big increase in pay, you'd better be prepared to show your company what it's going to get for the money. Long gone are the days when an employee asks a boss for a raise in pay because he or she is going to get married or going to have a baby. Today's bosses are fighting for survival. They're going head to head with the toughest international competition that they've ever known. They are not going to give you a raise in pay because they like you or because you need the extra money. And cost-of-living increases are miniscule!

In negotiating we say that there is magic in the power of trading off. Children know it instinctively. Your 6-year-old says, "I fixed your computer for you, Mom. Do you want to go to the movies tonight?" Your 10-year-old says, "I washed your car for you, Dad. Can we go to Chuck E. Cheese's tonight?" Children know that it's a lot easier to get somebody to do something if you offer something in return.

Look how much trouble unions have getting employers to make concessions when they don't offer anything in return. The supermarket clerks union, which is the United Food and Commercial Workers union, went on strike in Southern California. The employers, in effect, told the union workers that this job is no longer worth $15 an hour and that they could no longer afford expensive healthcare packages for everyone. They could replace the union workers with a machine that would work 24/7 and won't need any healthcare coverage.

When the dust settled several months later, machines had replaced several thousand workers, no increases in pay were given, and healthcare coverage had been slashed. If only the union had realized how much easier it would have been using the magic of trading off. If only the union had said, "We're going to give you the most highly motivated, highly trained employees in the world. You won't have to worry about finding them, training them, motivating them, or disciplining them. We're going to do all that for you!" When you offer something in return, it's much easier to get your employer to agree to your request for a big increase.

Develop a plan that shows your employer what you're going to do for him or her next year. Tell him all the wonderful things you're going to do for him in that new position. Convince your manager that you're going to be a huge success that will make the company money and make her look good, too. Have her salivating at the thought of all the things you're going to do. Only when you've done that are you ready to start your negotiation.

If it's appropriate, suggest working for a percentage of the gross profit increase. Employers hate to do it, but it's a great negotiating strategy. We use this close at the Power Negotiating Institute when we have employers balking at what they perceive to be the high cost of our training. "First of all," we tell them, "negotiating training doesn't cost, it pays. Second, we'd love to do it for no cash up front. Just pay us a percentage of the increase in profit that we make for you." For a moment, that sounds good to the company president, but he or she quickly thinks, "I could end up paying them a fortune if I agree to that, and it's far too convoluted to figure it all out." What we've done is put our money where our mouth is in convincing him or her that negotiating doesn't cost; it pays. The company will quickly agree to pay the fee.

Key Points to Consider:

- Don't try to manipulate an employer into giving more than you're worth. Sell him on how much extra money you're going to make for him, and he'll be glad to share a part of it with you.
- Offer to work for a share of the increased profits. Employers hate to do it, but offering means that you're putting your money where your mouth is.

Chapter 36 ▸▸▸

Negotiating a Raise in Pay Can Be Nerve-Racking

Let's face it: Sitting down and negotiating an increase in pay with your boss isn't a thing anyone looks forward to. It's a tense negotiating situation. It's tense because so many personal power factors come into play. Four of them really come into play when you're negotiating for more money:

- ▷ Title Power.
- ▷ Reward Power.
- ▷ Coercive Power.
- ▷ Information Power.

Title Power

The first power that can be nerve-racking is title power. You are dealing with someone who has a more powerful position than you, and that can be intimidating. We respect titles and professional designations in this country, not as much as the Swiss and the Germans do, but to a great extent. We feel intimidated when we negotiate a raise in pay with a vice president in charge of Human Resources.

What settles your nerves on this issue is remembering that some of these titles don't mean a thing. My daughter Julia graduated from the University of Southern California with a business-finance degree and went to work as a financial consultant for Dean Witter in a huge Beverly Hills office.

She hadn't been there long before she was talking about becoming a vice president at Dean Witter. I told her, "Julia, you've got to set realistic goals in life. That's a huge corporation and it may take you years and years to become a vice president. "Oh, no," she told me, "I think I'll be a vice president by the end of the year."

"Good lord, how many vice presidents does Dean-Witter have?"

"I don't know. It must be thousands. We've got 35 in this one office."

Don't be intimidated because the person with whom you are negotiating has a fancy title. It may not indicate any real power at all.

Reward Power

The second intimidating element when interviewing is Reward Power. Because the HR director has the ability to reward you by giving you a pay increase, it makes you feel very vulnerable.

Don't focus on how much you need the raise. Concentrate on the thought that there are dozens of companies out there willing to pay you well for your skills. If you're prepared to put all of your talents on the line to solve your company's problems, you are rewarding your company; the company is not rewarding you.

If you do your job so well that your company would have no idea how to replace you, you are rewarding the company by being willing to accept a pay raise when you could do so much better by working for another company.

Coercive Power

Coercive Power is the power to punish. What if they get angry with you because you ask for a raise? What if they get so upset that they accuse you of lack of loyalty to the company?

Many years ago when I was president of a large real estate company in Southern California, the owner of the company, Bruce Mulhearn, needed constant reassurance that I was loyal to him, which I was. The problem was that we had different biological clocks. He was always at his desk by six o'clock in the morning and in bed by nine in the evening. I prefer to work late at night and definitely see no point in confusing my day by having two six o'clocks in it.

One morning I wandered into my office at a little after nine and he was waiting for me, so upset that his veins were popping out of his forehead.

"You know Roger, I don't think that you have any loyalty to me at all."

This wasn't a good way to start the day. "Of course I'm loyal to you," I reassured him, "Why, I'd come to work in a dress if you wanted me to."

"I don't want you to come to work in a dress," he screamed at me, "I just want you here at the same time I get to work in the morning."

I gave it a long pause, and finally said, "I really had my heart set on the dress!"

He finally burst out laughing, we went off to get some coffee, and he never questioned my work schedule again.

Hopefully, you'll think of that story if your boss questions your loyalty because you had the nerve to ask for a raise in pay, and the silliness of it all will make you smile and overcome your anxiety.

Information Power

Chances are you're sitting there wondering what they know that you don't know. Is the company in an expansion mode where it's looking for good people to move up in the organization? Or is it downsizing, where it's in financial difficulties and looking for ways to cut payroll—maybe eliminating your job? When information is withheld, it makes us nervous and uptight.

Many companies use this as a weapon to control their employees. They have information that is restricted to the management, not because it's that secretive, but because they know that withholding information can intimidate the employees.

Ignore all that corporate nonsense and have the courage to ask for what you're worth.

Key Points to Consider:

Four personal power factors come into play when you're asking your boss for a raise in pay:

- Title Power. Don't be intimidated just because your boss has a fancy title.
- Reward Power. Focus on how much you're going to reward your company, not how much you need the company to reward you.
- Coercive Power. Don't be intimidated from fear that they have the power to fire, demote, or humiliate you.
- Information Power. Not knowing makes us anxious, so the more you know about your company, the more self-confident you become.

Chapter 37 ▸▸▸

Never Negotiate With Someone Who Can Only Say No to You

When negotiating for a raise in pay you should never negotiate with someone who can only say no to you. That's an underlying principle of negotiating, isn't it? There's no point in trying to negotiate a better deal with a store clerk if the store clerk doesn't have the authority to say yes to you. There's no point in negotiating for a loan at a bank with a bank officer who can only say no to you. And the same thing applies with negotiating an increase in pay with your boss. Obviously, you have to go through channels. If your boss is the office manager, it wouldn't be very smart of you to go around her and just walk into the office of the vice president in charge of operations, sit down, and start talking about an increase in pay! However, understand the dimensions of what's going on. If you were only talking to the office manager and the office manager has to get this increase in pay approved by the vice president, chances are the office manager is working on a very tight budget. There is pressure on her to keep expenses down and if she feels she can retain you without having to give you an increase in pay, chances are she'd prefer not to do that. That puts you in the awkward situation of having to put pressure on her, to get her to take that request of an increase in pay to her boss.

Putting pressure on her in this situation very often means threatening to quit, in one way or another, and that creates confrontation—which creates bad feelings, and gets the office manager down on you. So your first thought should be, "Can the person that I'm going to sit and talk to about this increase in pay give me an okay right away, or does he or she have to go to somebody else higher up the company chain of command?" If he or she doesn't have the authority to give you the increase in pay, then you have three alternatives:

1. Go over his or her head.
2. Request that you sit down with your immediate supervisor and the person who could give the increase in pay.
3. Work through your immediate supervisor, but get him or her on your side in terms of getting you the increase in pay.

Let's look at each of these three options:

First, going over your immediate supervisor's head is very dangerous. In most corporations, it will backfire on you. It could always be an option later, if you fail to get what you want and you're willing to quit over it. However, in the initial stages of the negotiation, let's rule that one out.

Option number two is to request a meeting between you, your supervisor, and his or her boss to discuss this increase. Whether you'd want to do this or not depends a lot on the personality of your immediate supervisor. If he doesn't have a very strong personality, he may actually appreciate the fact that you're willing to go with him and state your case. However, if he's very protective of his department, he may really be opposed to this because he feels he'd be losing some power over his department. I'd suggest that you consider the personality of your immediate supervisor and, if you're not sure how he'd feel about this suggestion, just put it to him. Say, "What will be the best way for us to handle this? Would you like me to come with you, or would you prefer to go to the boss yourself?"

The third alternative always seems the best one to me and that's to work with your immediate supervisor to get him or her on your side so she will sincerely work to get you what you want. To make this work best for you, be sure that you review the Higher Authority technique that I'll teach you in Chapter 48. There are two counter gambits that are very important here. When your boss tells you that he or she has to get your raise in pay approved by somebody else, your first response should always be to appeal to that person's ego. You say, "But he always goes along with your suggestions, doesn't he?" If you've got a boss with a big ego, she won't be able to resist this. She'll say. "Why yes, you're right, it's really just a formality. He always does what I want him to do." But sometimes the response will be, "Oh, yes, he normally goes along with my suggestions, but I can't approve it without his say so." Then you'd go to counter gambit number two, which is to get her commitment that she'll recommend it to the higher authority: "And you will recommend this increase to him, won't you?" By pinning her down in this way, she can only go one of two ways. Of course, the hopeful response is, "Well, yes, I think you've earned the increase. I'll do everything I can to get it for you." But in the back of her mind, she wasn't willing to recommend you enthusiastically for the increase. This technique will bring it out. At that point she'll say, "Well, frankly, I think he's going to want to see an improved performance from you, before he'll approve this." Any time you can draw out an objection, you're ahead, because it gives you an opportunity to answer, and counter that objection.

So a basic principle of negotiating an increase in pay is to never negotiate with someone who can only say no to you.

Key Points to Consider:

- Never negotiate with someone who can only say no to you.
- Avoid going over your boss's head.
- Ask you boss if you'd like him to go with you to negotiate the increase with his boss.
- Sell your boss on selling the increase to her boss by appealing to your boss's ego: "Your boss always follows your recommendations, doesn't he?"

Chapter 38 ▶▶▶ Anticipating Objections

First, anticipate and preclude objections that might come up in the negotiation. The two standard objections you're going to hear when you ask for an increase in pay are:

- ▷ The company isn't doing well enough to afford the increase in pay.
- ▷ Your performance isn't good enough to get an increase in pay.

Let's discuss these one at a time. First, the company isn't doing well enough to afford the increase in pay. Come to the conference loaded down with information about this one. If your company is publicly traded, spend an evening on the Internet researching the company's performance. Because of access to the Internet, so much information is available that would have been hard to locate in the past. Look for stock trends, press releases that tout good performance by the company, investments made in expansion, and so on.

Preempt your boss from the "we can't afford it" defense by talking about the company's performance. "Isn't it great to be working for a company that's doing so well," you start out with. "The stock is up 9 percent over the last nine months. Sales are up 12 percent and profits are better than ever."

Then the "your performance isn't good enough to get an increase in pay" argument. Hopefully this is not true. Come to the session armed with details about the goals you set for your performance last year and how you accomplished nearly all of them. Tell your boss, "Having you work on setting these goals for me was very helpful last year. After you've approved my raise in pay, I'm looking forward to doing it again this year."

If you didn't accomplish your goals, come up with a plausible reason why it wasn't your fault. "The only thing that stopped us from accomplishing all these goals was the company cutting back on funding for our department."

Key Points to Consider:

Anticipate the two big objections to giving you a raise:

- The company isn't doing well enough. Counter this by starting with a review of how well the company is doing.
- Your performance isn't good enough. Counter this by coming prepared with proof of the way you have met your goals and made the company more money.

Chapter 39 ▸▸▸

Concentrate on the Issues

A negotiating gambit that really comes into play here is learning to concentrate on the issues. Think of it as a game of tennis. The ball is being hit back and forth across the net. The only thing that affects the outcome of the game of tennis is the movement of the ball across the net. Good tennis players concentrate on the ball—not on what the other player is doing! And when you're negotiating for an increase in pay, the only thing that matters is the movement of the goal concessions across the negotiating table. The only thing that matters is "where are we now, compared to where we were five minutes ago, half an hour ago, yesterday, or last week."

Because in our minds we very quickly tie how much money we make to our worth as a human being, we're in very sensitive territory here. Things may be said in this negotiation that would cause you get angry and upset with the other person. It may even cause you to quit on the spot and stomp out. Be prepared for this kind of sensitive issue. Good negotiators don't let themselves get upset in a negotiation. International arms negotiators only walk out of a negotiation as a planned negotiating gambit. The only time they ever allow themselves to get upset is as a planned negotiating gambit.

Former Secretary of State Warren Christopher says, "It's okay to get upset with people in a negotiation, as long as you're in control and you're doing it as a specific negotiating technique. It's when you get upset and lose control that you always lose in a negotiation."

You should take the same approach in negotiating an increase in pay with your boss. Have your objective be clear, think through your negotiating strategy, and implement that strategy. Focus on results, not emotions. Don't get derailed if your boss criticizes your performance or questions your loyalty. The only thing you should focus on is this: Where are we now compared to five minutes ago or 30 minutes ago? Be a good negotiator and learn to concentrate on the issues.

Key Points to Consider:

- Concentrate on the issues when you're negotiating, not the personalities.
- Don't take it personally. Just because someone is critical of the job you've done, doesn't mean that he or she is critical of you as a human being.
- It's okay to get upset when you're negotiating, but don't lose control of yourself.

Part Two

Negotiating Pressure Points

If the employer is dragging his or her feet making you a job offer or giving you a raise, it's time to get some action with the subtle use of negotiating pressure points. These are techniques that bring pressure to bear. They need to be used subtly so that the employer doesn't take offense or feel that you're being too aggressive in promoting your position. There are three major pressure points:

- ▷ Time Pressure.
- ▷ Information Power.
- ▷ Walk Away Power.

Chapter 40 ▸▸▸

Time Pressure

Time pressure plays a part in every negotiation, but it has special significance when you are negotiating compensation.

Your children know about time pressure, don't they? If they want something, when do they ask for it? Just at the last moment, right? Just when you are rushing out the door for an important meeting and you're already late—that's when they know they have the best chance of getting what they want. Why? Because it's easier to give it to them than to take time talking about it.

People become flexible under time pressure. When employers are not under any time pressure to get you on board, it's hard to negotiate a great compensation package. When they are under a lot of time pressure, you can often get a terrific compensation package.

What time pressures might the employer be under? Of course, you won't know until you have invested some time gathering information and asking questions, but here are some that come to mind:

- ▷ They want to promote the person who is doing the job now but can't until they find a replacement.
- ▷ The position has been open for a while and morale is sinking in the department, or the territory is not being serviced well.
- ▷ You have an expertise to solve a problem that is costing them money or giving them heartburn.

- ▷ The person who is doing the job now is failing, but they can't fire him until they find a replacement.
- ▷ The person doing the job now needs to give you on-the-job training and can't move on to her new job until you're hired.

This is just a partial list of the many things that could put the employer under time pressure. Make your own checklist and expand it with each new situation you encounter. Keep your list in mind when you first meet with the interviewer and see if you can spot any symptoms of time pressure he or she may be experiencing.

Acceptance Time

Understand that it often takes potential employers time to understand that the goals they set for this hire are unrealistic. It takes them time to realize that they're not going to get someone with a master's degree to take the job. It takes time for them to realize that they are going to have to pay more than they expected for someone with the experience that they want.

Perhaps they need time to see that they are not going to get a better applicant or get you to take what they've offered you. My advice is to always leave the door open for the employer to reopen negotiations. Instead of pressuring them by saying, "This is my final offer," leave the door open with statements such as, "I hope you find the person you're looking for, but if you don't, call me. If I haven't found what I'm looking for, we can always talk some more."

Spending a Lot of Time With the Employer

Patience is a real virtue when negotiating. The longer you can keep the employer involved in negotiations, the better chance you have of getting what you want. Take your time finding out about the company. Ask as many questions as you can think of. If you can get them to give you a tour of their facilities, make it last as long as you can. Why do these things? For two reasons:

1. The longer you spend with them, the more trust they will develop in you.
2. The more time they spend with you, the more flexible they will become when the negotiations start. Time spent with you will affect their flexibility on salary and other compensation factors. Why? Because mentally they want to recoup the time spent with you. Their mind starts to tell them, "I can't walk away from this empty-handed after all the time I have invested."

There is a caveat here. If you aren't careful, time can work against you in the negotiations as well. You may find yourself becoming more flexible for the same reasons employers do. Your subconscious mind will be saying, "I don't want to walk away from this with nothing after all the time I've spent on it."

Tie Up All the Details

Don't leave anything to "we can work that out later." Sometimes an issue comes up early on and neither side wants to slow down the negotiations by taking time to resolve it. Perhaps it's an issue of a moving expenses or amount of vacation the first year. The HR directors says, "That's not a problem; we can work that out later." Perhaps it wouldn't be a big problem if you worked it out now, but if you wait until you're ready to put the final deal together and you're under a lot of time pressure, it could become a deal-breaker. Or you're so intent on getting the job that you're not prepared to walk away over this issue and you have to concede it. My advice is to tie up all the details and avoid last-minute surprises.

Key Points to Consider:

- People under time pressure become flexible, so don't reveal your deadlines, but try to establish that the employer has a time deadline.
- The principle of Acceptance Time tells you that it may take time for the employer to accept how much he or she is going to have to pay you. Leave the door open for him or her to come back to you with a better offer.
- People become flexible in relationship to the time they have spent with you because they subconsciously want to recoup that investment of time. String it out as long as you can!
- Don't leave anything to "we can work that out later."

Chapter 41 ▸▸▸

Information Power

Gathering information is so important to a job applicant. When you think you know everything you need to know about an employment situation, you probably know about half of what you really need to know. Here's a checklist of some of things that are helpful to learn:

- ▷ How long have they been looking at applicants?
- ▷ When do they need the position filled?
- ▷ What happened to the previous person doing this job? Was he or she promoted or fired?
- ▷ How many qualified people have applied for the job?
- ▷ What would disqualify an applicant?

The more information you can learn about the employer and the situation, the better insight you will have into his or her real motivation for hiring someone. Any bit of information you learn could potentially lead to a creative win-win solution will help you get the job and improve your bargaining power.

Don't Be Afraid to Ask the Tough Questions

I used to be reluctant to ask tough questions for fear I would offend people. I used to preface my questions with statements such as, "Would you mind if I asked you…?" or "Would you be embarrassed to tell me...?" I've since learned to ask tough questions more directly, by professionally asking, "How much are you authorized to offer?" or "How much bonus did the previous person make?" Even if the HR director refuses to answer the questions, you're still gathering information. As a good investigative reporter does, even if he or she refuses to answer, you can learn a lot by judging his or her reaction to your questions. Don't limit your information gathering by only asking questions that you know the employer will answer.

People Share Information Across Peer Group Levels

People share information much more easily with people in their same peer group. Everybody has an allegiance not just to the company they work for but also the profession or occupation in which they see themselves. Let's say that you're a computer engineer and the HR director gives you a tour of the department, during which you get to chat with one of the computer engineers. You call him and ask to meet him for lunch the next day. You'll be able to get all kinds of information, because he sees himself in the same peer group as you.

Where You Ask the Question Makes a Difference

Note that in that example you asked the engineer to meet for lunch. Information flows a lot more freely out of the workplace. In the workplace, invisible chains of protocol surround employers and employees. They are sensitive to what they feel they should talk about and what they feel they shouldn't. Get them out of the work environment and information flows much more freely. Certainly if you could get that employer out for a game of golf or out to dinner, information would flow. But even if you can get them out of their office to their company lunchroom or across the street to Starbucks for a cup of coffee, information will flow much more readily.

Ask Open-Ended Questions

Rudyard Kipling once wrote about his six honest serving men. He said that these six taught him all he knew. Those six serving men were Who, What, Where, When, Why, and How. Today we recognize them as the first words of open-ended questions: questions phrased in such a way that their answers provide additional information. The opposite of these are closed-ended questions, which a simple yes or no can answer without giving any additional information. Let's look at the difference between open-ended and closed-ended questions that deal with salary negotiations:

Open-ended:

- What's the biggest hiring bonus you've ever paid?
- How flexible are you on your offer?

Closed-ended:

- Would you pay a hiring bonus if I came on board on the first of the month?
- Would you include a company car?

When you're trying to gather information, use open-ended questions. Open-ended questions keep the employer talking, and that relaxes him or her. This interview skill takes practice to perfect, but the better you become at it, the more information you will gather.

Key Points to Consider:

- The more information you can learn about the employer and his or her situation, the better insight you will have into his or her real motivation for hiring someone.
- Ask the tough questions. Even if he won't tell you, you're still gathering information.
- People share information across peer group levels. You can learn a lot from having a cup of coffee with someone who is in the same profession as you or who shares the same background.
- Information flows more freely away from the workplace where the other person is surrounded by invisible chains of protocol.
- Ask open-ended questions to draw out the other person.

Chapter 42 ▸▸▸

Projecting That You're Prepared to Walk Away

This is the most important pressure point of all. If you said, "I'm in a big rush because I've got a meeting with an employer in 15 minutes. Just give me one thing that will make me a more powerful negotiator," it would be, "Project to the employer that you're prepared to walk away if you can't get what you want."

Hundreds of people have come up to me at my seminars to ask me about salary negotiations. They are trying to get their boss to give them a raise in pay or they are being promoted or taking on more responsibility and they don't feel they have much power in the negotiation. Almost invariably they don't feel they have much power because they're not prepared to leave the company over it.

Walk Away Power is essential to your success in salary negotiations. When my daughter Julia bought her first car, she went down to the BMW dealership and test-drove a really nice used BMW. She fell in love with the car, and they knew she'd fallen in love with it.

When she got home, she asked me to go back with her and renegotiate a better price. On the way to the dealership, I asked her, "Are you prepared to come home tonight without the car?"

"No, I'm not!" Julia replied. "I want it! I want it!"

"If you feel that way," I told her, "you may as well give them what they want, because you've already set yourself up to lose. You've got to be prepared to walk away."

We spent two hours negotiating the purchase and even walked out of the showroom twice during those two hours, but finally they got the car for $2,000 less than Julia was prepared to pay. So, how much money was Julia making while she was negotiating...bearing in mind that I waived my normal fee? Two thousand dollars in two hours, right? A thousand dollars an hour! I'd call that pretty good money anywhere! And it just goes to show that you can't make money faster or easier than you can when you're negotiating.

Projecting that you're prepared to walk away is the number-one pressure point to use when negotiating with employers, but how do you give yourself Walk Away Power? You do it by giving yourself options. Before going into a negotiation, develop some options.

Research two other employment opportunities with which you'd be almost as happy. This doesn't mean that you're going to storm into your boss and say, "Give me what I want or I'm out of here," but it will make you a more powerful negotiator. Employers seem to be able to sense when you have other options, and this makes you a more powerful negotiator.

When you're negotiating compensation with a new employer, your compensation package can go up dramatically if you have one or more other employers making you offers. This really hit home to me in a negotiation with a book club. I have sold four of my books to major book clubs, so I know how much they pay. But once I got three times what I was expecting. Why? Because there was another book club bidding on the same book. Having options gives you power in a negotiation, so develop your options before you start negotiating.

Study these pressure points and try them out in small day-to-day negotiations. Practice them in situations that aren't important so you can perfect them for use in ones that are. Time Pressure, Information Power, and Walk Away Power are three powerful pressure points that, when used properly, will get you better deals in any salary negotiation.

Key Points to Consider:

- Convincing the employer that you're prepared to walk away is the number-one pressure point in any negotiation.
- You give yourself Walk Away Power before you go into the negotiation.
- Convincing a potential employer that you have other opinions will dramatically improve the offer he or she gives you.

Part Three

Negotiating Gambits

Gambit is a chess term that means any maneuver for advantage. If you play chess, you know that there are beginning gambits to get the game started in your direction, middle gambits to keep the momentum going, and ending gambits when you get ready to checkmate the other player or, in salary negotiating terms, seal the deal.

There are some other parallels between chess and negotiating. It only takes you an hour or two to learn chess gambits or negotiating gambits, but it might take you a lifetime to learn when to make those moves. Knowing when to use these gambits with an employer is every bit as valuable as knowing which gambit to use.

Both chess gambits and negotiating gambits can work even if the other side recognizes the gambit that you're using. Don't be concerned that the employer recognizes a gambit. He or she will admire your negotiating skills, and it's always more fun to negotiate with someone who knows how to negotiate!

Chapter 43 ▸▸▸ Ask for More Than You Expect to Get

One of the most important negotiating gambits is to have the courage to ask for more than you expect to get in the negotiations. If you're hoping to get a 10 percent increase in pay, you're better off to ask for a 20 percent increase in pay, and then be willing to back down from that position. If you're applying for a new job that offers $80,000 and you're thinking of asking for $100,000 and settling for $90,000, you're better off to ask for $110,000.

International negotiators say there are many more reasons for putting a proposal on the negotiating table than the thought that the other side might say yes. International negotiators often make outrageous demands even though they know the other side will never agree. They will give you three justifications for doing this:

1. It puts new pressure on the other side.
2. It expands the negotiating range so that any compromise seems to be a concession.
3. It gives you a chance to judge the other side's reaction to the proposal.

The same principles apply in asking for an increase in pay. When you ask for more than you expect to get, you put pressure on your boss that wasn't there before. You expand the negotiating range, which creates a climate where your boss can have a win in the negotiations, because when you ask for 20 percent and then back down to 10 percent, the compromise seems to be a concession. But more importantly, you've allowed your boss to have a win in the negotiation. He or she may even end up with the HR director saying to his or her boss, "Well, she asked me for a 20 percent increase, but I was able to negotiate her down to a 10 percent increase."

Henry Kissinger, Richard Nixon's Secretary of State and one of the top international negotiators of last century, went so far as to say: "Effectiveness at the bargaining table depends on your ability to overstate your initial demands."

Note that Kissinger says ability, meaning how well you can do it. Why do you think he said this so unequivocally? It seems like such a simply theory, but there are a lot of underlying reasons that make it one of the most powerful negotiating gambits of all. Here are five key reasons for overstating your initial demands:

1. You might just get it.
2. Asking for more makes it easier to get what you really want.
3. Asking for more raises your perceived value.
4. Asking for more creates a climate where the other side can have a win with you.
5. Asking for more than you expect to get prevents deadlocks when dealing with an egotistical person.

1. You Might Just Get It

If you're a positive thinker, that's probably the first thing that occurred to you. You might just get it, and the only way you're going to find out is to ask for it. It might just be your lucky day. It may be the day that all that rabbit-foot-stroking and charm-carrying pays off for you. And the only way you're going to find out is to ask!

There is a corollary to this principle: The less you know about the situation, the more you expand the negotiating range, for two reasons:

- ▷ You may be uninformed about what this employer is willing to pay. If you haven't researched pay scales and if you haven't done the thorough research you should, you may be way off in your estimates of what the job pays. You may think that $80,000 a year is pushing the envelope, while the employer expects to pay $95,000. If that's what the employer thinks the job is worth, he or she might refuse to hire someone who only asks for $80,000, assuming that such an applicant could not be qualified.
- ▷ If you're dealing with a stranger, you need to build rapport quickly. The fastest way to build rapport is to be able to make concessions. I agree that it's a long way from being the best way to build rapport, but it is the fastest.

2. Asking for More Makes It Easier to Get What You Really Want

I learned that from my eldest son, Dwight. One day at dinner he asked me if he could borrow my Corvette that evening. I was surprised he asked because I'd always had a rule that he couldn't drive it unless I was with him, but I didn't want to upset him so I couched my reply gently. "Dwight, that's a very fast car. I don't think I'd feel comfortable letting you drive it unless I'm with you. I'd hate to see you get hurt in an accident."

He looked really disappointed and said, "Could I borrow the minivan, then?" I wasn't too eager to let him do that either, but I thought about it for a while and then said, "Okay, I guess I don't have a problem with you doing that."

I didn't think anything of it until half an hour later I looked out into the driveway. Dwight plays bass guitar with a group of his friends, and he was loading two huge loudspeakers into the back of the minivan. "Wait a minute," I thought, "he evidently had no intention of borrowing my Corvette. He just knew to ask for more than you expect to get. It makes it a lot easier to get what you really want."

Is there a danger here? Can you blow yourself out of contention for a job by asking for too much? Yes, indeed. Employers are reluctant to hire an employee for less money than they request. They are afraid that the employee will be unhappy. They are the afraid that the employee will be too demanding for other increases. And they are afraid that the employee will take the job but leave for the first better-paying job that comes along.

If you're pushing the envelope on your demands, you need to imply some flexibility. Let's say that the employer has floated $80,000 as the ballpark figure for what the job pays. You'd like to get $100,00 but would settle for $90,000. Rather than asking for $90,000 with a take-it-or-leave-it attitude, I'd rather see you ask for $110,000 and imply some flexibility. Demanding $110,00 would be a mistake. If you demand $110,000 with a take it or leave it attitude, you may not even get the negotiations started. The employer may take you out of the running if there is no possibility of paying you that much. Imply some flexibility when you push the envelope. The employer asks you what it would take to get you on board and you reply, "Based on all the money I'm going to make you in this position I think that $110,00 would be reasonable figure for me to suggest." At that, the HR director will be thinking, "That's not going to fly, but this is my best candidate and it does sound as though there is some flexibility here. I'm going to spend some time negotiating with him and see what I can get him for."

3. Asking for More Raises Your Perceived Value

You need to tell the potential employer what you think you're worth and why. The higher the number, the more the perceived value. If the HR director asks you how much you want and you lack the courage to forcefully ask for what you feel you're worth, you immediately discount that perceived value.

Which applicant would you rather hire if you knew nothing else about them? You ask each applicant how much money they want and applicant A says, "I feel that I'm worth every penny of $100,000." Applicant B says, "I'd like to get $100,000 but I'll take $80,000 if that's all the job pays."

It's the same mistake that the salesperson makes when he or she drops the price too quickly. The buyer says, "Give me your best price." The salesperson responds with, "List price is $75 per widget, but I can give them to you for $65 if you'll give me the order today." See the mistake that has been made? He or she has immediately discounted the perceived value of the product and service. Don't do that when you're negotiating your compensation package! Leave that big number out there—in writing, if you can. That's one of the seven keys to credibility I talk about in my audio program "Secrets of Power Persuasion." People are more likely to believe what they see in writing than they are when they just hear it.

4. Asking for More Creates a Climate Where the Other Side Can Have a Win With You

This is the key issue for negotiators. This is why Henry Kissinger says, "Effectiveness at the bargaining table depends on your ability to overstate your initial demands." He's telling you to create a climate where the other side can have a win with you. If you go in with your very best offer up front, there is no way that the HR director can have a win with you. Inexperienced negotiators always want to do this. This is the salesperson who is saying to his or her sales manager, "I'm going out on this big proposal today. I know it's going to be competitive. They're talking to everyone else in town. Let me cut the price up front or we won't stand a chance of getting it." Experienced negotiators know the power of asking for more than they expect to get and imply flexibility if they are pushing the envelope. Create a climate where the other side can have a win with you and you'll find it much easier to get what you want.

5. Asking for More Than You Expect to Get Prevents Deadlocks When Dealing With an Egotistical Person

All I mean by egotistical is the HR director who is proud of his ability to negotiate. He likes nothing more than saying to his boss, "Here's an applicant who was asking for $100,000 and she's probably worth it, but I negotiated with her and she's happy to accept $75,000."

Remember the first Persian Gulf War? The United States made three demands of Saddam Hussein:

1. Get out of Kuwait.
2. Restore the legitimate government of Kuwait. Don't do what the Soviets did in Afghanistan and install a puppet government.
3. Make reparations for the damage you did.

Those were the three demands made by the United States. What's wrong with that? The problem is that it was also our bottom line. It was also the least we were prepared to settle for. No wonder it deadlocked! It had to deadlock! We didn't give Saddam Hussein, a very egotistical man, a chance to have a win. Why would we take that position? Are our State Department negotiators complete blithering idiots? I don't think so. I don't think that the United States had any intention of settling for those three things. General Schwarzkopf, who led the U.S. invasion of Kuwait, said this in his book, *It Doesn't Take a Hero*: "The minute we got down there, we understood that anything less than a military victory was a defeat for the United States." We couldn't let Saddam Hussein pull 600,000 troops back across the border and leave us wondering when he would choose to invade Saudi Arabia.

There's an example of a negotiation where we wanted to create a deadlock, because it served our purpose. What I'm concerned about is the possibility that you will inadvertently create a deadlock with your employer or potential employer because you don't feel comfortable with the concept of asking for more than you expect to get.

When you ask for more than you expect to get, be sure to smile as you ask. I can't remember where I first heard this piece of advice, but it has been worth its weight in gold. I think it was in a French film a decade or two ago where a man was teaching a child how to go into the marketplace and beg. "Whenever you ask for something, be sure to smile," he told him. What great advice. A smile says:

- I like you.
- This is going to be fun.
- You don't have to worry because this is not going to be confrontational.
- Don't be offended, because I'm not expecting you to do anything you don't want to do.
- If you want to make a counter-proposal, I would be happy to listen to it.

Smile when you ask for something. Isn't that great advice? It works when you're trying to seduce someone. It works when you're trying to negotiate a better deal. And it definitely works when you're asking an employer to pay you more than you think you'll get.

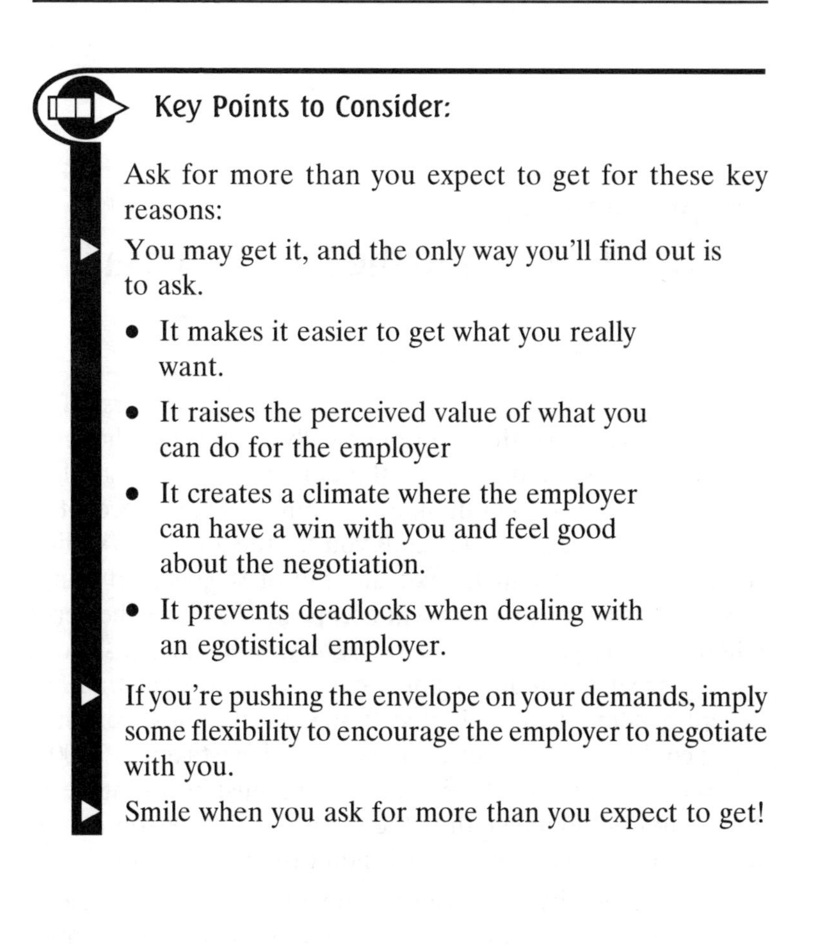

Key Points to Consider:

Ask for more than you expect to get for these key reasons:

- You may get it, and the only way you'll find out is to ask.
  - It makes it easier to get what you really want.
  - It raises the perceived value of what you can do for the employer
  - It creates a climate where the employer can have a win with you and feel good about the negotiation.
  - It prevents deadlocks when dealing with an egotistical employer.
- If you're pushing the envelope on your demands, imply some flexibility to encourage the employer to negotiate with you.
- Smile when you ask for more than you expect to get!

Chapter 44 ▸▸▸

Don't Say Yes to the First Proposal

The reason that you should never say yes to the first offer (or counter-offer) is that it automatically triggers two thoughts in the person's mind. Perhaps the employer is making a low offer to you but doesn't think for a moment you will accept it. The employer desperately needs you for the job and is willing to pay $100,000. He makes you an offer of $80,000, not thinking for a moment that you will accept it. How does he react when you say yes? His first thought would not be, "Wow, what a great negotiator I am. I could not have got them to accept a penny less." His first thought will almost certainly be, "I could have done better. They would have taken $75,000." His second thought will be, "Something must be wrong here. I must not be understanding the picture if this person is willing to say yes to an offer that I didn't think she would."

Let's apply that to a common negotiating situation. Let's say that you're thinking of buying a second car. The people down the street have one for sale, and they're asking $10,000. That is such a terrific price on the perfect car for you that you can't wait to get down there and snap it up before somebody else beats you to it. However, on the way there you start thinking that it would be a mistake to offer them what they're asking, so you decide to make a super-low offer of $8,000 just to see what their reaction is. You show up at their house, look the car over, take it for a short test-drive, and then say to the owners, "It's not exactly what I'm looking for, but I'll give you $8,000."

You're waiting for them to explode with rage at such a low offer, but what actually happens is that one spouse looks at the other and says, "What do you think, dear?" And the spouse says, "Let's go ahead and get rid of it."

Does this exchange make you jump for joy? Does it leave you thinking, "Wow, I can't believe what a deal I got! I couldn't have gotten it for a penny less"?

I don't think so. I think you're probably thinking:

1. "I could have done better."
2. "Something must be wrong."

Apply that concept to a salary negotiation with your current employer. You ask for a 20 percent increase. Your boss tells you that he or she can only afford a 10 percent increase, but she is thinking that she can afford 15 percent if she had to. But you jump at the 10 percent.

At this point, your boss is thinking:

1. "I could have done better. If he were happy with 10 percent, he probably would have taken 5 percent."
2. "Something is going on that I don't understand if he is willing to take less than I thought he would."

In the hundreds of seminars that I've conducted over the years, I've posed a situation such as this to audiences, and can't recall getting anything other than these two responses. Sometimes people reverse them, but usually the response is automatic: "I could have done better" and "Something must be wrong."

Let's look at each of these responses separately:

First Reaction: I could have done better. The interesting thing about this is that it doesn't have a thing to do with the price. It has to do only with the way the other person reacts to the proposal. What if you'd offered $7,000 for the car, or $6,000, and they told you right away that they'd take it? Wouldn't you still think you could have done better? What if one of your employees asked you for a 10 percent increase in pay, but jumped at your counter-offer of 5 percent? Wouldn't you still think you could have done better?

Second Reaction: Something must be wrong. The second thought you'd have when the seller of that car said yes to your first offer is that something must be wrong.

Those two reactions will go through anybody's mind if you say yes to the first offer. Let's say your son came to you and said, "Could I borrow the car tonight?" and you said, "Sure, son, take it. Have a wonderful time." Wouldn't he automatically think, "I could have done better. I could have gotten $10 for the movie out of this"? And wouldn't he automatically think, "What's going on here? Why do they want me out of the house? What's going on that I don't understand"?

This is a very easy negotiating principle to understand, but it's very hard to remember when you're in the thick of tense salary negotiation and the proposal the employer makes is better than you expected it to be. Here's the mistake that you have made. You may have formed a mental picture of how you expect the employer to respond, and that's a dangerous thing to do. Napoleon Bonaparte once said, "The unforgivable sin of a commander is to 'form a picture'—to assume that the enemy will act a certain way in a given situation, when in fact his response may be altogether different." So you're expecting him or her to counter at a ridiculously low figure and to your surprise the other person's proposal is much more reasonable than you expected it to be. For example:

> *You have finally plucked up the courage to ask your boss for an increase in pay. You've asked for a 15 percent increase in pay, but you think*

> *you'll be lucky to get 10 percent. To your astonishment, your boss tells you that he or she thinks you're doing a terrific job, and he or she would love to give you the 15 percent increase in pay that you're asking for. Do you find yourself thinking what a wonderfully generous company this is that you work for? I don't think so. You're probably wishing you'd asked for a 25 percent increase.*

Power Negotiators are careful that they don't fall into the trap of saying yes too quickly, which automatically triggers in the other person's mind:

1. I could have done better. (And next time I will. A sophisticated person won't tell you that he felt that he lost in the negotiation; but he will tuck it away in the back of his mind, thinking "The next time I deal with this person I'll be a tougher negotiator. I won't leave any money on the table next time.")
2. Something must be wrong.

Turning down the first offer may be tough to do, particularly if it's taken you weeks to pluck up the courage to ask for more.You will be tempted to grab what you can. When this happens, be a Power Negotiator—remember not to say yes too quickly.

Key Points to Consider:

Never say yes to the first offer or counter-offer from the other side. It automatically triggers two thoughts:

- I could have done better. (And next time I will.)
- Something must be wrong.

Chapter 45 ▶▶▶ Flinch at the First Proposal

Power Negotiators know that you should always *flinch*—react with shock and surprise—when your potential employer makes the first proposal.

Let's say that you are in a resort area and stop to watch one of those charcoal sketch artists. He doesn't have the price posted, so you ask him how much he charges, and he tells you $15. If that doesn't appear to shock you, his next words will be, "And $5 extra for color." If you still don't appear shocked, he will say, "And we have these shipping cartons here, you'll need one of these too."

Perhaps you know someone who would never do anything similar to that because it's too theatrical. The kind of person who would walk into an art gallery and say, "How much is the sculpture in the window?"

"$22,000."

"That's not bad!" they say.

I know it sounds dumb and I know it sounds ridiculous, but the truth of the matter is that when that human resources director makes a proposal to you, he or she is watching for your reaction. She may not think for a moment that you'll go along with her suggestion. She's just throwing it out to see what your reaction will be. For example, she asks you if you'll go to work for the same amount you were making on your last job, and she may not think for a moment that you would go along with the request, but if you don't *flinch*, she will automatically think, "Maybe I will get her to go along with that. I didn't think she would, but I think I'll be a tough negotiator and see how far I can get her to go."

It's very interesting to observe a negotiation when you know what both sides are thinking. Wouldn't that be fascinating for you? Wouldn't you love to know what's going on in your employer's mind when you're negotiating with him or her?

When I conduct the all-day or two-day Secrets of Power Negotiating seminars, we break up into groups and do some negotiating to practice the principles that I teach. I create a workshop and customize it to the industry in which the participants are involved.

I break the audience up into buyers, sellers, and referees. The referees are in a very interesting position, because they have been in on the planning sessions of both the buyers and the sellers. They know each side's negotiating range. They know what the opening offer is going to be, and they know how far each side will go.

The referees might see the buyers make a proposal to the sellers that they know the buyers think is an outrageously low proposal. They barely have the nerve to propose it. They think that they are going to get laughed out of the room the minute they do. To their surprise the sellers don't appear to be that shocked by their offer. They thought the sellers were going to yell, "You want us to do what? You must be out of your mind. We're not going to do that!" Instead the sellers' response is much more moderate. They calmly respond, "I don't think that we'd be prepared to go that low." In an instant, the negotiation changes. What a moment ago was a ridiculously low offer now seems doable. You can see the change in the buyers' faces. Now the buyers are thinking, "Perhaps we're not as far apart as we thought we were."

Let's create a situation for a salary negotiation. Let's say that Chris is applying for a position as marketing director at a company that makes laptop computers. The job encompasses all internal communications between the company, its employees, and its dealers. There will be newsletters to write, contests to create and implement, and network communications to manage throughout North America. The employer is thinking that he or she will have to pay $100K to $150K to get a good person. There's also the possibility that the company could expand the job to include communications with its advertising agencies. If the company did that, it could pay up to $200K.

Chris, the applicant, is not a perfect match for the job, but has good credentials and has earned $100K for similar work in the past. He's had an offer at $150K, but it would involve moving from Orange County, California, to New York, and he doesn't want to do that.

Chris is now being called in for a third interview and is on the short list. It's time to start talking about money. He's going to ask for $150K but he's afraid that the employee will be shocked at that and it will put him out of consideration.

"You're one of the people that we're seriously considering for this position," the HR director tells Chris. "What would it take to get you on board? Would you be willing to start at the $100K you were making if we agree to review it in six months based on the job you're doing for us?"

Chris braces for rejection and says, "I've already been offered $150K for a similar position. I was assuming that we'd be talking at least that much."

Chris believes $150K is ridiculously high, barely has the nerve to propose it, and fears being laughed out of the room. However, to Chris's surprise, the HR director doesn't appear to be that shocked. Chris is afraid he's going to say, "You want us to do what? You must be out of your mind." What the HR director actually responds with is much milder—perhaps,

"I don't think we'd be prepared to go that high." In an instant, the negotiation changes. A moment ago, the $150K had seemed to be an impossible goal. Now Chris is thinking that perhaps they're not as far apart as Chris thought they were. Now Chris is thinking, "Let's hang in. I'm going to be a tough negotiator. Maybe I will get that much."

Remember that if the employer suggests a range, you only respond to the high end of the range. Ignore the low end. They tell you, "The job will pay in the $60,000 to $70,000 range." You should ignore the low-end figure and only flinch at the high end. "Wow, I was expecting much more than $70,000!" you say.

Flinching is critical because most people believe what they see more than what they hear. The visual overrides the auditory in most people. It's safe for you to assume that at least 70 percent of the people with whom you negotiate will be visuals. What they see is more important than what they hear. I'm sure you've been exposed to some neuro-linguistic programming. You know that people are visual, auditory, or kinesthetic (what they feel is paramount). There are a few gustatory (taste) and olfactory (smell) people around, but not many, and they're usually chefs or perfume blenders.

If you'd like to know what you are, close your eyes for 10 seconds and think of the house in which you lived when you were 10 years old. Assuming that you're not driving a car or operating heavy equipment, go ahead and do that now.

If you're a visual, you saw the house in your mind, you got a picture of it. At my seminars at least 70 percent of the attendees are visual, and sometimes as much as 90 percent.

Perhaps you didn't get a good visual picture, but you heard what was going on, perhaps trains passing by or children playing. That means you're auditory. Neil Berman is a psychotherapist friend of mine in Santa Fe, New Mexico. He's very auditory. He can remember every conversation he's ever had with a patient, but if he meets a patient in the supermarket, he doesn't remember him or her. The minute she says good morning to him, he thinks, "Oh yes, that's the bi-polar personality with anti-social tendencies."

The third possibility is that you didn't so much see the house, or hear what was going on, but you just got a feeling for what it was like when you were 10 years old. That makes you a kinesthetic.

Assume that people are visual unless you have something else to go on. Assume that what they see has more impact than what they hear. That's why it's so important to respond with a *flinch* to a proposal from the other side.

Don't dismiss *flinching* as childish or too theatrical until you've had a chance to see how effective it can be. It's so effective that it usually surprises my students when they first use it.

A woman told me that she *flinched* when selecting a bottle of wine in one of Boston's finest restaurants and the wine steward immediately dropped the price by five dollars. A man told me that a simple *flinch* caused the salesperson to take $2,000 off the price of a car.

Key Points to Consider:

- *Flinch* in reaction to a proposal from the other side. They may not expect to get what they're asking for, but if you don't show surprise you're communicating that it's a possibility.
- A concession often follows a *flinch*. If you don't *flinch*, it makes the other person a tougher negotiator.
- Assume that the other person is a visual unless you have something else on which to go.
- Even if you're not face to face with the other person you should still gasp in shock and surprise. Telephone *flinches* can be very effective.

Chapter 46 ▸▸▸ Don't Be Confrontational

What you say in the first few moments of a salary negotiation often sets the climate of the negotiation. Your boss or prospective employer quickly gets a feel for whether you are working for a win-win solution, or whether you're a tough negotiator who is out for everything you can get.

That's one problem that I have with the way that attorneys negotiate: They're very confrontational negotiators. You get that white envelope in the mail with black, raised lettering in the top left hand corner and you think, "Oh no. What is it this time?" You open the letter and what's the first communication from that attorney? It's a threat. What he's going to do to you, if you don't give him what he wants.

Be careful what you say at the beginning. Arguing always intensifies the other person's desire to prove him or herself right. Confrontation creates competition. You're much better off to agree with the other person initially and then turn it around using the Feel, Felt, Found formula.

You start a negotiation with your boss for an increase in pay, only to be told, "We're going through the toughest times this industry has ever seen. We're all lucky to be working here."

Respond with, "I understand exactly how you **feel** about that. Many other people have **felt** exactly the same way as you do right now. (Now you have diffused that competitive spirit. You're not arguing with him; you're agreeing with him.)

But you know what I have always **found**? When times are tough it's also a time of great opportunity. Let me tell you some of the ideas I have for getting us past these difficult times."

Let's say that you are applying for a job and the human resources director says, "I don't think you have enough experience in this field." If you respond with "I've handled much tougher jobs than this in the past," it may come across as, "I'm right and you're wrong." You're going to force her to defend the position she's taken. Instead, say, "I understand exactly how you feel about that. Many other people would feel exactly the same way as you do right now. However, there are some remarkable similarities between the work I've been doing and what you're looking for that are not immediately apparent. Let me tell you what they are."

So instead of arguing up front, which creates confrontational negotiation, get in the habit of agreeing and then turning it around.

Try this exercise yourself and see the response you get: Ask two people to stand facing each other. Tell one that he has a diamond in the palm of his hand. Tell him to clench his fist around it. Then tell the other person to do anything she can to get the diamond from the first person. Chances are that the second person will grab the other person's fingers and try to pry them off the diamond. This creates confrontation and makes the first person fight to protect the diamond. Rarely will the second person say, "Please give me the diamond." Confrontation creates competition.

Another great thing about Feel, Felt, Found is that it gives you time to think. You're expecting your boss to be reasonably receptive to your request for an increase in pay. Unfortunately, you catch him at a bad moment. He laughs and says, "I can't believe you've got the nerve to ask me after the miserable job you've done for us this year!" You don't know what to say; but if you have Feel, Felt, Found in the back of your mind, you can say, "I understand exactly how you feel about that. Many other people would feel exactly the same way in your position. However, I have always found...." By the time you get there, you'll have thought of something to say.

Key Points to Consider:

- Don't argue with people in the early stages of the negotiation because it creates confrontation.
- Use the Feel, Felt, Found formula to turn the hostility around.
- Having Feel, Felt, Found in the back of your mind gives you time to think when the other side throws some unexpected hostility your way.

Chapter 47 ▶▶▶

The Vise Gambit

The Vise is another very effective negotiating gambit, and what you can accomplish with it will amaze you. The Vise Gambit is the simple little expression: "You'll have to do better than that."

Here's how Power Negotiators use it:

You're an advertising account executive with a great reputation handling nationwide advertising accounts for imported automobiles. An advertising agency on Madison Avenue has been courting you for months and is finally ready to make you an offer.

You're bracing yourself for a low offer, but the proposal the agency makes is better than you dared to expect, and it includes a healthy commission on any accounts you bring with you.

Instead of jumping at the offer, you respond with the Vise Gambit by calmly saying, "I'm sorry. You'll have to do better than that."

An experienced negotiator will automatically respond with the Counter Gambit, which is, "Exactly how much better than that do I have to do?" trying to pin you down to a specific. However, it will amaze you how often inexperienced negotiators will concede a big chunk of their negotiating range simply because you did that.

What's the next thing that you should do, once you've said, "You'll have to do better than that"?

You have it. **Shut Up!** Don't say another word. This is the Silent Close that I taught you earlier. The other side may just make a concession to you. Salespeople learn the silent close during the first week they are in the business. You make your proposal and then shut up. The other person may just say yes, so it's foolish to say a word until you find out if he or she will or won't.

I once watched two salespeople do the Silent Close on each other. There were three of us sitting at a circular conference table. The salesman on my right wanted to buy a piece of real estate from the salesman on my left. He made his proposal and then shut up, just as they taught him in sales training school. The more experienced salesperson on my left must have thought, "Son of a gun. I can't believe this. He's going to try the Silent Close on *moi*? I'll teach him a thing or two. I won't talk either."

I was sitting between two strong-willed people who were both silently daring the other to be the next one to talk. There was dead silence in the room, except for the grandfather clock ticking away in the background. I looked at each of them and, obviously, they both knew what was going on. Neither one was willing to give in to the other. I didn't know how this was ever going to get resolved. It seemed as though half an hour went by, although it was probably closer to five minutes. Finally, the more experienced salesperson broke the impasse by scrawling "DECIZION?" on a pad of paper and sliding it across to the other. He had deliberately misspelling the word *decision*. The younger salesperson looked at it and without thinking said, "You misspelled decision." And once he started talking, he couldn't stop. (Do you know any salespeople who act that way? Once they start talking, they can't stop?) He went on to say, "If you're not willing to accept what I offered you, I might be willing to come up another $2,000;

but not a penny more." He re-negotiated his own proposal before he found out if the other person would accept it or not.

So to use the Vise Gambit, Power Negotiators simply respond to the other side's proposal or counter-proposal with, "I'm sorry, you'll have to do better than that." And then shut up.

A client called me up after a Secrets of Power Negotiating seminar that I had conducted for his managers and told me, "Roger, I thought you might like to know that we just made $14,000 using one of the Gambits that you taught us. We are having new equipment put into our Miami office. Our standard procedure has been to get bids from three qualified vendors and then take the lowest bid. So I was sitting here going over the bids and was just about to okay the one I'd decided to accept. Then I remembered what you taught me about the Vise technique. So I thought, 'What have I got to lose?' and scrawled across it, 'You'll have to do better than this,' and mailed it back to them. The counter-proposal came back $14,000 less than the proposal that I was prepared to accept."

You may be thinking, "Roger, you didn't tell me whether that was a $50,000 proposal, in which case it would have been a huge concession, or a multi-million dollar proposal, in which case it wouldn't have been that big a deal." Don't fall into the trap of negotiating percentages when you should be negotiating dollars. The point was that he made $14,000 in the two minutes that it took him to scrawl that counter-proposal across the bid. Which meant that, while he was doing it, he was generating $420,000 per hour of bottom-line profits. That's pretty good money, isn't it?

This is another trap into which attorneys fall. When I work with attorneys, it's clear that, if they're negotiating a $50,000 lawsuit, they might send a letter back and forth over $5,000. If it's a million-dollar lawsuit, they'll kick $50,000 around as though it doesn't mean a thing, because they're mentally negotiating percentages, not dollars.

If you're a salesperson and you make a $2,000 concession to a buyer, it doesn't matter if it got you a $10,000 sale or a million-dollar sale. It's still $2,000 that you gave away. So it doesn't make any sense for you to come back to your sales manager and say, "I had to make a $2,000 concession, but it's a $100,000 sale." What you should have been thinking was, "$2,000 is sitting in the middle of the negotiating table. How long should I be willing to spend negotiating further to see how much of it I could get?"

Have a feel for what your time's worth. Don't spend half an hour negotiating a $10 item (unless you're doing it just for the practice). Even if you got the other side to concede all of the $10, you'd be making money only at the rate of $20 an hour for the half-hour you invested in the negotiation. To put this in perspective for you, if you make $100,000 a year, you're making about $50 an hour. You should be thinking to yourself, "Is what I'm doing right now generating more than $50 per hour?" If so, it's part of the solution. If you're aimlessly chatting with someone at the water cooler, or talking about last night's television movie, or anything else that is not generating $50 an hour, it is part of the problem.

Here's the point. When you're negotiating with an employer—when you have a deal in front of you that you could live with—but you're wondering if you could hang in a little bit longer and do a little bit better, you're not making $50 an hour. No way. You're making $50 a minute and probably $50 a second.

And if that's not enough, remember that in salary negotiations it means even more than that. Let's say that you use Power Negotiating skills to get your new employer to pay you just $50 more a week, which is a very modest goal. It's not just $50. It's $50 a week for as long as you work for that organization. Every future increase will be based on that higher amount. If you only work for that organization for five years, it amounts to $13,000 more to you. If it took you 30 minutes to negotiate the increase, you were making $26,000 an hour while you were negotiating. That's pretty good money by anybody's standards!

Power Negotiators always respond to a proposal with, "You'll have to do better than that." And when the other person uses it on them, they automatically respond with the Counter Gambit: "Exactly how much better than that do I have to do?"

Key Points to Consider:

- Respond to a proposal or counter-proposal with the Vise Gambit: "You'll have to do better than that."
- If it's used on you, respond with the Counter Gambit: "Exactly how much better than that do I have to do?" This will pin the other person down to a specific.
- Concentrate on the dollar amount that's being negotiated. Don't think percentages.
- A negotiated dollar is a bottom-line dollar. Be aware of what your time is worth on an hourly basis.
- You will never make money faster than you will when you're Power Negotiating.

Chapter 48 ▸▸▸
Pressure Without Confrontation

One of the most frustrating situations you can run into while trying to negotiate a salary is with the HR person who claims that he or she doesn't have the authority to make a final decision. Unless you realize that this is simply a negotiating tactic that's being used on you, you'll have the feeling that you'll never get to talk to the real decision-maker.

When I was president of the real estate company in California, I used to have salespeople coming in to sell me things all the time: advertising, photocopy machines, computer equipment, and so on. I would always negotiate the very lowest price that I could, using all of these gambits. Then I would say to them, "This looks fine. I do just have to run it by my board of directors, but I'll get back to you tomorrow with the final okay."

The next day I could get back to them and say, "Boy, are they tough to deal with right now. I felt sure I could sell it to them, but they just won't go along with it unless you can shave another couple of hundred dollars off the price." And I would get it. There was no approval needed by the board of directors, and it never occurred to me that this deception was underhanded. The people with whom you deal see it as well within the rules by which one plays the game of negotiating.

So when the HR person says to you that they have to take it to the employment committee or the executive committee, it's probably not true, but it is a very effective negotiating tactic.

Let's first look at why this is such an effective tactic, and then I'll tell you how to handle it when they use it on you.

Why the Employer Loves to Use Higher Authority

You would think that if you were going out to negotiate something, you would want to have the authority to make a decision. At first glance it would seem that the HR person would have more power if he or she were able to say to the applicant, "I have the authority to make a deal with you."

Power Negotiators know that you put yourself in a weakened negotiating position when you do that. The HR director is better off to tell you that he or she has to check with a hiring committee for approval. He has to put his ego on the backburner to do this, but it is very effective.

Higher Authority works much better when the higher authority is a vague entity, such as a committee or a board of directors. For example: Have you ever actually met a loan committee at a bank? I never have. Bankers at my seminars have consistently told me that for loans of $500,000 or less, somebody at that bank can make a decision without having to go to loan committee. However, the loan officer knows that if she said to you, "Your package is on the president's desk," you would say, "Well, let's go talk to the president right now. Let's get it resolved." You can't do that with a vague entity.

The HR director will probably make the higher authority a vague entity such as a committee, because the committee seems unapproachable to you. If he told you that his manager would have to approve it, what's the first thought that you're going to have? Right. "Then why am I wasting time talking to you? If your manager is the only one who can make a decision, get your manager down here." However, when your higher authority is a vague entity, it appears to be unapproachable. In all the years at the real estate company telling people that

I had to run it by my board of directors, I only once had someone say to me, "When does your board of directors meet? When can I make a presentation to them?"

The use of Higher Authority is a way of putting pressure on people without confrontation. If the HR director says, "I'm not going to pay you that much," it is confrontational. When he or she says, "I can't get approval for that much," it's non-confrontational.

Higher Authority is a very effective way of pressuring people without confrontation. I'm sure you can see why employers love using it on you. Look at the benefits to them when they tell you that they have to get your salary and benefits package approved by a committee:

- ▷ They can put pressure on you without confrontation: "We'd be wasting our time taking a proposal that high to the committee."
- ▷ It unbalances you as a negotiator because it's so frustrating to feel that you're not able to present to the real decision-maker.
- ▷ By inventing a higher authority, they can set aside the pressure of making a decision.
- ▷ It sets them up for using the Vise Gambit: "You'll have to do better than that if you want to get it past the committee."
- ▷ It puts you in the position of needing the other person to be on your side if it's to be approved by the committee.
- ▷ They can make suggestions to you without implying that it's something to which they'd agree: "If you can come down another 10 percent, you may have a chance of the committee approving it."

- ▷ It can be used to force you into a bidding war: "The committee has asked me find five acceptable applicants. If you're asking for the most money it wouldn't rule you out, but it would put you at a disadvantage."
- ▷ The other person can squeeze your price without revealing what you're up against: "The committee is meeting tomorrow to make a final decision. Being more flexible on your pay and benefit requirements would improve your chances."
- ▷ It sets the other person up to use Good Guy/Bad Guy: "If it were up to me, I'd love to get you on board, but the bean counters on the committee care only about the best deal."

The Counter-Gambits to Higher Authority

You can see why employers love to use the Higher Authority Gambit on you. Fortunately, Power Negotiators know how to handle this challenge smoothly and effectively.

Your first approach should be trying to remove the other person's resort to higher authority before the negotiations even start, by getting her to admit that she could make a decision if the proposal was irresistible. This is exactly the same thing that I taught the real estate agents to say to the buyers before putting them in the car, "Let me be sure I understand. If we find exactly the right property for you today, is there any reason why you wouldn't make a decision today?" It's exactly the same thing that the car dealer will do to you when, before he lets you take it for a test drive, he says, "Let me be sure I understand. If you like this car as much as I know you're going to like it, is there any reason why you wouldn't make a decision today?" Because they know that if they don't remove the resort to higher authority up front, then there's a danger that under the pressure of asking for a decision, the other person will invent a higher authority as a delaying tactic, such as, "Look, I'd love to give you a decision today, but I can't because my father-in-law has to look at the property (or the car) or Uncle Joe is helping us with the down payment and we need to talk to him first."

One of the most frustrating things that you encounter is the HR director saying to you, "Well, that's fine. Thanks for bringing me the proposal. I'll talk to our executive committee about it and if they are interested we'll get back to you." Where do you go from there? If you're smart enough to counter the Higher Authority Gambit before you start, you can remove yourself from that dangerous situation.

Let's say that you've interviewed three times for a position as head of emergency care at an inner city hospital. They have told you that you're their number-one choice and they would like you to present a proposal to them. Your objectives in presenting your proposal to them should be:

1. Communicate that you have options, which gives you power in the negotiation.
2. Remove the HR director's resort to higher authority.

Before you present your proposal to the HR director, before you even get it out of your briefcase, you should casually say, "I don't mean to put any pressure on you. (*That's called a preparer. You have just given yourself permission to put pressure on them.*) But I am considering another offer (*You're communicating that you have options, which gives you power.*) They are pressuring me for a decision. Let me ask you this: If this proposal meets **all of your needs** (*That's as broad as any statement can be, isn't it?*), is there any reason why you wouldn't give me a decision right away?"

It's a harmless thing for the HR director to agree to because the other person is thinking, "If it meets all of my needs? No problem, there's loads of wiggle room there." However, look at what you've accomplished if you can get him or her to respond with, "Well, sure if it meets *all* of our needs, I'll give you an okay right now." Look at what you've accomplished:

1. You've eliminated their right to tell you that they want to think it over. If they say that, you say, "Well, let me go over it one more time. There must be something I didn't cover clearly enough because you did indicate to me earlier that you were willing to make a decision today."
2. You've eliminated their right to refer it to a higher authority. You've eliminated their right to say, "I want our legal department to see it, or the hiring committee to approve it."

What if you're not able to remove their resort to higher authority? I'm sure that many times you'll say, "If this proposal meets all of your needs is there any reason why you wouldn't give me a decision today?" and the HR director will reply, "I'm sorry, but this is a key position and everything has to get approved by the executive committee. I'll have to refer it to them for a final decision."

Here are the three steps that Power Negotiators take when they're not able to remove the other side's resort to higher authority:

- ▷ Appeal to the other person's ego.
- ▷ Get the other person's commitment that he'll recommend it to the higher authority.
- ▷ Use the qualified "Subject To" Close.

Step 1: Appeal to the Other Person's Ego

With a smile on your face you say, "But they always follow your recommendations, don't they?" With some personality styles that is enough of an appeal to the ego that he'll say, "Well, I guess you're right. If I like it, then you can count on it." But often he'll still say, "Yes, they usually follow my recommendations, but I can't give you a decision until I've taken it to the committee."

(If you realize that you're dealing with an egotistical person, try preempting his resort to higher authority early in your presentation, by saying, "Do you think that if you took this to your manager, she'd approve it?" Often an ego-driven person will make the mistake of proudly telling you that he doesn't have to get anybody's approval.)

Step 2: Get the Other Person's Commitment That He'll Recommend It to the Higher Authority

So you say, "But you will recommend me to them—won't you?" Hopefully, you'll get a response similar to, "Yes, it looks good to me. I'll go to bat for you with them."

Getting the other side's commitment that he's going to recommend it to the higher authority is very important, because it's at this point that he may reveal that there really isn't a committee. He really does have the authority to make a decision and saying that he had to check with someone else was just a negotiating gambit that the company was using on you.

In Step 2, Power Negotiators get the other person's commitment that she will go to the higher authority with a positive recommendation. There are only two things that can happen now: Either she'll say yes, she will recommend it to them, or she'll say no, she won't. Either way you've won. Her endorsement would be preferable, of course, but any time you can draw out an objection you should say, "Hallelujah" because objections are buying signals. People are not going to object to your proposal unless they are interesting in hiring you.

Objections are buying signals. We knew in real estate that if we were showing property, and the people were "oohing and aaahing" all over the place, if they loved everything about the property, they weren't going to buy. The serious buyers were the ones who were saying, "Well, the kitchen's not as big as we like. Hate that wallpaper. We'd probably end up knocking out that wall." Those were the ones who would buy.

If you're in sales, think about it. Have you ever in your life made a big sale where the person loved your price up front? Of course not. All serious buyers complain about the price.

Your biggest problem is not an objection—it's indifference. Let me prove this to you. *Give me the opposite of the word love*. If you said hate, think again. As long as they're throwing plates at you, you have something there with which you can work! It's indifference that is the opposite of love. You should be worried when they say, as Rhett Butler did in *Gone with the Wind*, "Quite frankly, my dear, I don't give a damn." That's when you know the movie is over. Indifference is your problem, not objections. Objections are buying signals.

So when you say to them, "You will recommend it to them, won't you?" they can either say yes, they will, or no, they won't. Either way, you've won. Then you can move to Step 3.

Step 3: Use the qualified "Subject To" Close

The qualified "Subject To" Close in this instance would be: "Then you'll hire me if I pass your physical?" or "Do we have a deal, subject to your verifying my application?" or "So once you've received my college transcript, we have a deal?"

To review, the three steps to take if you're not able to get the other person to waive his or her resort to higher authority are:

1. Appeal to the other person's ego.
2. Get the other person's commitment that he'll recommend it to the higher authority.
3. Use the qualified "Subject To" Close.

Using Higher Authority to Put Pressure on the Employer

Higher authority is a great way to put pressure on the employer without confrontation. If you say, "I'm not going to work for that little," it's very confrontational. Better that you say, "I'm very excited about going to work for you because I know I can do a sensational job for you. Frankly, that's more important to me than the money involved. But, with a wife and two children in college, I don't always get to do what I want to do. I can discuss it with them but I don't think they'll go along with it unless you can afford the number I suggested to you." Now you're putting pressure on the employer without confrontation.

What's the counter to the Counter-Gambit? What if someone was trying to remove your resort to higher authority in that way? If the other person says to you, "You do have the authority to make a decision, don't you?" you should say, in so many words, "It depends on what you're suggesting. If you can agree to my proposal, I can make a decision. Anything less than that I'll have to discuss with my family."

One more thing about the Higher Authority Gambit. What if you have an employer who is trying to force you to decide before you're ready to make a decision?

Let's say that you're applying for a job as assembly line foreperson at a manufacturing plant. They're saying to you, "We want you for the job, but this is what it pays. Give me a decision now, or I'm going to go with the next person in line."

How do you handle it? Very simple. You say, "I'm happy to give you a decision. In fact, I'll give you an answer right now if you want it. But I have to tell you—if you force me to a decision now, the answer has to be no. Tomorrow, after I've had a chance to talk to my family, the answer might be yes. So why don't you wait until tomorrow and see what happens? Fair enough?" Don't let people rush you into making a decision that you may regret later.

You may find yourself in a situation in which escalating authority is being used on you. You think that you have cut a deal, only to find that the head of personnel has to approve it and won't. You sweeten the deal only to find that the vice president won't give approval. Escalating authority is in my mind outrageously unethical, but you do run into it. I'm sure that you've experienced it when trying to buy a car. After some preliminary negotiation, the salesperson surprises you by immediately accepting your low offer. After getting you to commit to a price (which sets you up psychologically to accept the idea that you will buy that car), the salesperson will say something such as, "Well, this looks good. All I have to do is run this by my manager and the car is yours."

You can feel the car keys and ownership certificate in your hands already, and you are sitting there in the closing room congratulating yourself on getting such a good deal, when the salesperson returns with the sales manager. The manager sits down and reviews the price with you. He says, "You know, Fred was a little out of line here." Fred looks properly embarrassed. "This price is almost $500 under our factory invoice cost." He produces an official-looking factory invoice. "Of course, you can't possibly ask us to take a loss on the sale, can you?"

Now you feel embarrassed yourself. You're not sure how to respond. You thought you had a deal, and Fred's higher authority just shot it down. Unaware that the dealer could sell you the car for 5 percent under invoice and still make money because of factory incentives, you fall for the sales manager's appeal to your being a reasonable person and nudge your offer up by $200. Again you think you've bought the car, until the sales manager explains that, at this incredibly low price, he needs to get his manager's approval. And so it goes. You find yourself working your way through a battalion of managers, each one able to get you to raise your offer by a small amount.

If you find the other side using escalating authority on you, remember these Counter-Gambits:

- ▷ You can play this game also, by bringing in your escalating levels of authority. The other person will quickly catch on to what you're doing and call a truce.
- ▷ At each escalating level of authority you should go back to your opening negotiating position. Don't let them close you by letting each level of authority cut off another slice of your compensation package.
- ▷ Don't think of it as a firm deal until you have final approval and the ink is dry on the contract. If you start mentally spending the increase in pay, you'll be too emotionally involved in the process to walk away.
- ▷ Above all, don't get so frustrated that you lose your temper and walk away from what could be a profitable transaction for everybody. Sure, the tactic could be deemed unfair, but you're there to grease the wheels of commerce, not to convert the sinners.

Being able to use and handle the resort to higher authority is critical to you when you're Power Negotiating. Always maintain your own resort to higher authority. Always try to remove the other person's resort to a higher authority.

Key Points to Consider:

- ▶ Don't let the other side know that you have the authority to make a decision.
- ▶ Your higher authority should be a vague entity, not an individual.

- Leave your ego at home when you're negotiating. Don't let the other person trick you into admitting that you have authority.
- Attempt to get the other person to admit that he or she could approve your proposal if it meets all of his or her needs. If that fails, go through the three counter gambits:
  - Appeal to his or her ego.
  - Get his or her commitment that he or she will recommend you to his or her higher authority.
  - Go to a qualified "Subject To" Close.
- If the other side is forcing you to make a decision before you're ready to do so, offer to decide but let him know that the answer will be no, unless he gives you time to check with "your people."
- If he or she is using escalating authority on you, revert to your opening position at each level and introduce your own levels of escalating authority.

Chapter 49 ▸▸▸

Don't Offer to Split the Difference

In the United States, we have a tremendous sense of fair play. Our sense of fair play dictates to us that if both sides give equally, then that's fair. If Fred puts his home up for sale at $400,000, Susan makes an offer at $380,000, and both Fred and Susan are eager to compromise, both of them tend to be thinking, "If we settled at $390,000 that would be fair, because we both gave equally."

Maybe it's fair and maybe it isn't. It depends on the opening negotiating positions that Fred and Susan took. If the house is really worth $380,000 and Fred was holding to his over-inflated price only to take advantage of Susan having falling in love with his house, then it's not fair. If the house is worth $400,000 and Susan is willing to pay that, but is taking advantage of Fred's financial problems, then it isn't fair. Don't fall into the trap of thinking that splitting the difference is the fair thing to do when you can't resolve a difference in price with the other side.

With that misconception out of the way, let me point out that Power Negotiators know that Splitting the Difference does not mean splitting it down the middle. Just split the difference twice and the split becomes 75 percent/25 percent; furthermore, you may even be able to get the employer to split the difference three or more times.

Here's how this gambit works:

The first thing to remember is that you should never offer to split the difference yourself, but always encourage the employer to offer to split the difference.

Let's say that you're an information technology specialist and you're being considered for a job as IT manager at a medium-sized retail chain. You have asked for $86,000 and they have offered $75,000. You've been negotiating for a while, during which time you've been able to get the employer up to $80,000, and you've come down to $84,000. Where do you go from there? You have a strong feeling that if you offered to split the difference they would agree to do so, which would mean agreeing at $82,000.

Instead of offering to split the difference, here is what you should do. You should say, "Well, I guess this is just not going to fly. It seems like such a shame though, when we've both spent so much time working on this. It seems like such a shame that it's not going to go together, when we're only $4,000 apart."

If you keep stressing the time that you've spent on it and the small amount of money that you're apart on the price, eventually the employer will say, "Why don't we split the difference?"

You act a little dumb and say, "Let's see, splitting the difference, what would that mean? I'm at $84,000 and you're at $80,000. What you're telling me is you'd come up to $82,000? Is that what I hear you saying?"

"Well, yes," he says. "If you'll come down to $82,000, then we'll settle for that." In doing this you have immediately shifted the negotiating range from $80,000 to $84,000. The negotiating range is now $82,000 to $84,000, and you have yet to concede a dime.

So you say, "$82,000 sounds a lot better than $80,000. Tell you what. Let me talk to my family (*or whatever other higher authority you've set up*) and see how they feel about it. I'll tell them you came up to $82,000, and we'll see if we can't put it together now. I'll get back to you tomorrow."

The next day you get back to him and you say, "I spent all last night talking about this with my family. They insist that we can't make it if we go a penny below $84,000. But we're only $2,000 apart on this now. Surely, we're not going to let it all fall apart when we're only $2,000 apart?"

If you keep that up long enough, eventually he'll offer to split the difference again.

If you are able to get him to split the difference again, this gambit has made you an extra $1,000 times the number of years you work for the company. However, even if you can't get him to split the difference again and you end up at the same $82,000 that you would have done if *you* had offered to split the difference, something very significant happened here. What was the significant thing that happened?

Right. They think they won because you got them to propose splitting the difference at $82,000. Then you got your family to reluctantly agree to a proposal the employer had made. If you had suggested splitting the difference, then you would have been putting a proposal on the table and forcing them to agree to a proposal that you had made.

That may seem to be a very subtle thing to you, but it's very significant in terms of who felt they won and who felt they lost.

Remember that the essence of Power Negotiating is to always leave the other side feeling that he or she won.

So the rule is never offer to Split the Difference, but always encourage the other person to offer to Split the Difference.

Key Points to Consider:

- Don't fall into the trap of thinking that splitting the difference is the fair thing to do.
- Splitting the difference doesn't mean down the middle, because you can do it more than once.
- Never offer to split the difference yourself; instead encourage the employer to offer to split the difference.
- By getting him to offer to split the difference, you put him in a position of suggesting the compromise. Then you can reluctantly agree to his proposal, making him feel that he won.

Chapter 50 ▶▶▶

Don't Take on Their Problems

Don't let other people give you their problems. If your boss, for example, says to you, "Well, we'd love to give you an increase in pay, but we just don't have it in the budget." Whose problem is that? It's not your problem that they didn't budget effectively for the increase you've worked for and deserve. It's their problem that they didn't budget effectively. Don't let them give you their problems. The standard response I teach is that when somebody tries to give you his or her problem you must test the problem for validity right away. You need to find out if this really is a deal-killer that she's given you, or just something she put on the negotiating table to see what your reaction would be. If she says to you, "We just don't have it in the budget." You say, "Well, who would have the authority to exceed the budget?" Remind her that a budget is simply a number written on a piece of paper and that number can be changed.

If you ask for a hiring bonus and she says to you, "That's not in our procedure!" you should respond with, "Who has the authority to change procedure at your company?" Procedure is just something written on a piece of paper somewhere, and if someone wrote it, someone can change it.

I remember negotiating a seminar for an HMO with its training director. She had agreed to my speaking fee, and my next objective was to sell her a set of audio programs for each attendee. There would be 80 people there and the programs sell for $70 each, so it would mean $5,600 more gross income to me. I told her, "You really should invest in an audio program for each of your people so they will continue to learn Power Negotiating even after the seminar is over." She told me, "That does sound like a good idea but unfortunately we don't have it in the budget."

She had just given me what was essentially her problem so I knew to test for validity. "When does your budget year end?"

"The end of September," she told me.

"So you would have it in the budget on October 1st?"

"Yes, I suppose we would."

"Then it's not a problem. I'll ship you the programs and bill you on October 1st."

"That would be fine," she told me.

Sometimes problems simply fall away when you know to test for validity.

I remember staying at the Anchorage Hilton hotel in Alaska to do a program for the AGC of Alaska—that's the Associated General Contractors, the people who build office buildings and hotels. I'd finished my morning seminar and needed to rest up for the long flight back to Los Angeles, so I went to the front desk and asked them to give me a 6 o'clock checkout. There were two young people standing next to each other behind the desk and one of them said, "Mr. Dawson, we could do that but we'd have to charge you an extra half day."

She had handed me a procedural problem created by the hotel, so I knew to test for validity. I said, "Who would have the authority to waive that charge?"

She pointed at the young lady next to her and said, "She would!"

I said to the supervisor, "How would you feel about waiving that charge?"

And she said, "Sure, we can do that. No problem."

Any time the employer tries to give you what is essentially his or her problem, learn to test it for validity right away. You need to find out if it's really a deal-killer or just something he or she threw out on the negotiating table to see what your response would be.

Let's practice some responses:

"We never pay hiring bonuses."

"What else could we call it?"

"I can't approve two weeks' vacation in the first year."

"Who could make an exception?"

"We only pay moving expenses for someone already on the payroll."

"Why don't you hire me here and then transfer me?"

Key Points to Consider:

- Don't let the employer pass on his or her internal problems to you. Test for validity right away.
- Testing for validity tells you whether the problem she tried to give you is a deal-killer or just something she threw out to test your reaction.
- Don't take objections at more than face value. Because she doesn't have it in the budget now doesn't mean she won't have it in the budget next month.
- Company procedure is written on paper, not chiseled in stone. Somebody wrote it, so somebody can change it.

Chapter 51 ▸▸▸

Trading Off

The Trade-Off Gambit tells you that anytime the other side asks you for a concession in the negotiations, you should automatically ask for something in return. Let's look at a couple of ways of using the Trade-Off Gambit:

- ▷ You're a physician and you're being promoted to head of your department at your hospital. The president says to you, "Would you be willing to sit on the ethics committee?" You respond with, "If I did that for you, what would you do for me?"
- ▷ You're negotiating a compensation package for your new job as regional manager for a company that engineers components for original equipment manufacturers. They ask you, "We may occasionally ask you to train new salespeople for other regions." You say, "If I do that for you, what will you do for me?"
- ▷ You're a successful real estate agent being promoted to office manager. The broker says to you, "I'd like you to teach one training class a month at our new agent's school. It'll give you good exposure to the new agents." You respond with, "If I did that for you, what would you do for me?"

When you ask for something in return, three things could happen:

1. **You might just get something.** It's not the real reason for doing it, but it could happen. You might get a fee or compensating time off.
2. **By asking for something in return, you elevate the value of the concession.** When you're negotiating, why give anything away? Always make the big deal out of it. You may need that later. Later on, you're asking a favor from him and if he balks, you can say, "I didn't give you a problem when you asked me to (sit on that committee, train those salespeople, or teach that class). Don't give me a problem with this. Fair enough?" When you elevate the value of the concession, you set it up for a trade-off later.
3. **It stops the grinding away process.** This is the key reason why you should always use the Trade-Off Gambit. If she knows that every time she asks you for something, you're going to ask for something in return, then it stops her from constantly coming back for more. So many times a student of mine has come up to me at seminar or called my office and said to me, "Roger, can you help me with this? I thought I had a sweetheart of a compensation package put together. I didn't think that I would have any problems at all with this one. But in the very early stages, they asked me for a small concession. I was so happy to have the opportunity that I told them, 'Sure, we can do that.' A week later they called me for another small concession, and I said, 'All right, I guess I can do that, too.' Ever since then, it's been one darn thing after another. Now it looks as though it's not that great an opportunity after all." This student should have known up front that when the other person

asked for that first small concession, he should have asked for something in return. "If I can do that for you, what can you do for me?"

I trained the top 50 salespeople at a Fortune 50 company that manufactures office equipment. The company has what they call a Key Account Division that negotiates its largest accounts with its biggest customers. These people are heavy-hitters. A salesperson at the seminar had just made a $43 million sale to an aircraft manufacturer. (That's not a record. When I trained people at a huge computer manufacturer's training headquarters in New York, a salesperson in the audience had just closed a $3 billion dollar sale—and he was in my seminar taking notes!)

This Key Account Division had its own vice president, and he came up to me afterwards to tell me, "Roger, that thing you told us about trading off was the most valuable lesson I've ever learned in any seminar. I've been coming to seminars like this for years and thought that I'd heard it all, but I'd never been taught what a mistake it is to make a concession without asking for something in return. That's going to save us hundreds of thousands of dollars in the future."

Please use these gambits word for word the way that I'm teaching them to you. If you change even a word, it can dramatically change the effect. If, for example, you change this from, "If we can do that for you what can you do for us?" to "If we do that for you, you will have to do this for us," you have become confrontational. You've become confrontational at a very sensitive point in the negotiations—when the other side is under pressure and is asking you for a favor. Don't do it. It could cause the negotiation to blow up in your face.

You may be tempted to ask for a specific concession because you think that you'll get more that way. I disagree. I think you'll get more by leaving the suggestion up to the other side.

Jack Wilson, who produced my video training tapes, told me that soon after I taught him this gambit, he used it to save several thousand dollars. A television studio called him and told him that one of its camera operators was sick. Would Jack mind if the studio called one of the camera operators that Jack had under contract and ask him if he could fill in? It was just a courtesy call. Something that Jack would have said "no problem" to in the past. However, this time he said, "If I do that for you, what will you do for me?" To his surprise, the studio said, "Tell you what. The next time you use our studio, if you run overtime, we'll waive the overtime charge." It had just conceded several thousand dollars to Jack, on something that he never would have asked for in the past.

When you ask what they will give you in return, they may say, "Not a darn thing," or "You get to keep your job, that's what you get." That's fine, because you had everything to gain by asking and you haven't lost anything. If necessary, you can always revert to a position of insisting on a trade-off by saying, "I don't think I'd feel comfortable agreeing to that without some form of compensation" or "Unless you're willing to give me compensating time off."

I would go so far as to say that you shouldn't make any concession to the employer unless you get something in return. It doesn't have to be something of equal value, but you need to get something. If you make a concession and don't get anything in return, you've cut your price and discounted the perceived value of your service or employment. You're a price-cutter. If you get something in return, even if it's not of equal value, you're a negotiator.

Creating Your Own Trade-Offs

If you sense that the employer is having a problem with a part of what you're proposing, look for acceptable trade-offs that you can propose. My friend Syd Bezonsky tells me that when he first went into insurance sales, there was a very high turnover of people. New salespeople would accept the draw the company offered, but when the draw ended and they went onto straight commission they would quit. Syd told the company, "I don't want a draw. If I can't sell, you shouldn't be paying me. Here's what I'll do: I work on straight commission from day one. All I ask in return is that you pay me 8 percent instead of 5 percent commission and assure me that however much money I make you won't complain or cut my territory." They jumped at the opportunity and soon Syd was making more than the president of the company. The company had a problem with Syd making that much money, but he was able to remind them of the deal that they had made.

Key Points to Consider:

- When asked for a small concession by the other side, always ask for something in return.
- Use this expression: "If I can do that for you, what can you do for me?"
- You may just get something in return.
- It elevates the value of the concession so that you can use it as a trade off later.
- Most important, it stops the grinding away process.
- Don't change the wording and ask for something specific in return because it's too confrontational.
- Don't make a concession unless you receive something in return. That makes you a negotiator, not a price-cutter.
- To get around objections, look for issues that you can trade off.

Chapter 52 ▸▸▸

Good Guy/Bad Guy

Good Guy/Bad Guy is one of the best known negotiating gambits. Charles Dickens first wrote about it in his book *Great Expectations*. In the opening scene of the story, the young hero, Pip, is in the graveyard, when out of the sinister mist comes a large, very frightening man. This man is a convict, and he has chains around his legs. He asks Pip to go home (convenient to the story, Pip's guardian was a blacksmith) and bring back food and a file, so he can remove the chains. The convict has a dilemma, however: He wants to scare the child into doing as he's asked, yet he mustn't put so much pressure on Pip that he'll be frozen in place or bolt into town to tell the policeman.

The solution to the convict's problem is to use the Good Guy/Bad Guy Gambit. Taking some liberty with the original work, what the convict says, in effect, is, "You know, Pip, I like you and I would never do anything to hurt you. But I have to tell you that waiting out here in the mist is a friend of mine and he can be violent, and I'm the only one who can control him. If I don't get these chains off—if you don't help me get them off—then my friend will come after you and hurt you. So, you have to help me. Do you understand?" Good Guy/Bad Guy is a very effective way of putting pressure on people, without confrontation.

I'm sure you've seen Good Guy/Bad Guy used in the old police movies. Officers bring a suspect into the police station for questioning, and the first detective to interrogate him is a rough, tough, mean-looking guy. He threatens the suspect with all kinds of things that they're going to do to him. Then he's mysteriously called away to take a phone call, and the second detective, who's brought in to look after the prisoner while the first detective is away, is the warmest, nicest guy in the entire world. He sits down and makes friends with the prisoner. He gives him a cigarette and says, "Listen kid, it's really not as bad as all that. I've rather taken a liking to you. I know the ropes around here. Why don't you let me see what I can do for you?" It's a real temptation to think that the Good Guy is on your side when, of course, he really isn't.

Then the Good Guy would go ahead and close on what, if you've read the earlier section on closing tactics, you would recognize as a Minor Point Close. "All I think the detectives really need to know is," he tells the prisoner, "where did you buy the gun?" What he really wants to know is, "Where did you hide the body?"

Starting out with a minor point such as that and then working up from there, works very well, doesn't it? The HR director says to you, "If you did join us, when could you start?" "Would you want to transfer over your 401(k) savings plan?" Little decisions lead to big ones. It's the real estate salesperson who asks you, "If you did invest in this home, how would you arrange the furniture in the living room?" Or "Which of these bedrooms would be the nursery for your new baby?" Little decisions grow to big decisions.

Bill Richardson, our former United Nations ambassador, tells this story about General Cedras, the dictator of Haiti, using Good Guy/Bad Guy: "With General Cedras of Haiti, I learned that he played good guy and that a top general, Philippe Biamby, played bad guy. So, I was prepared. During our meeting, Biamby leaped up on the table and started screaming, 'I don't like the U.S. government to call me a thug...Je ne suis pas un thug.' I remember turning to Cedras as Biamby was doing this and saying, 'I don't think he likes me very much.' Cedras laughed and laughed. He said, 'All right, Biamby, sit down.'"

People use Good Guy/Bad Guy on you much more than you might believe. Look out for it anytime you find yourself dealing with two people. Chances are you'll see it being used on you, in one form or another.

For example, you may sell industrial equipment and have been interviewing with the top manufacturer of drives for robotic assembly lines. It's a great job that pays a first-class salary and year-end bonus based on company profits. You've survived three rounds of interviews with the HR director and now have an appointment to meet with her again, along with the vice president of marketing. When she leads you in to meet with the vice president, you find to your surprise that the president of the company wants to sit in on the interview.

Now you're outnumbered three to one, so you feel intimidated, but you go ahead and everything appears to be going along fine. You feel that you have a good chance of getting the job, until the president suddenly starts getting irritated. Eventually he says to his vice president, "Look, I don't see any way that we could afford the kind of money he's talking about. I'm sorry, but I've got things to do." Then he storms out of the room.

This really shakes you up if you're not used to negotiating. Then the vice president says, "Wow. Sometimes he gets that way, but I really think you'd do well here and I think we can still work this out. If you could be a little more flexible on your compensation request, then I think we can still put it together. Tell you what—why don't you let me see what I can do for you with the president?"

If you don't realize what they're doing to you, you'll hear yourself say something along the lines of, "What do you think the president would agree to?" Then it won't be long before you'll have the vice president negotiating for you—and he or she is not even on your side.

If you think I'm exaggerating on this one, consider this: Haven't you, at one time or another, said to a car salesperson, "What do you think you could get your sales manager to agree to?" As if the salesperson is on your side, not on the sales manager's? Haven't we all at one time been buying real estate and have found the property we want to buy, so we say to the agent who has been helping us find the property, "What do you think the sellers would take?" Let me ask you something: Who is your agent working for? Who is paying her? It's not you, is it? She is working for the seller, and yet she has effectively played Good Guy/Bad Guy with us. So, look out for it, because you run into it a lot.

This gambit is very effective even when everybody knows what's going on. It was how Presidents Carter and Reagan got the hostages out of Iran, wasn't it? In November 1980, the voters kicked Jimmy Carter out of office. The Iranians were still holding our state department employees hostage in our embassy in Tehran. Carter was eager to secure their release before he left the White House and Reagan could take credit for their release. So, he started playing Good Guy/Bad Guy with the Ayatollah. He said to him, "If I were you, I'd settle this thing with me. Don't take a chance on this new team coming into office in January. My goodness, have you taken a look at these guys? The president's a former cowboy actor. The vice president is the former head of the CIA. The secretary of state is Alexander Haig. These guys are crazier than Englishmen. There's no telling what they might do."

Reagan, playing along with it, said, "Hey, if I were you, I'd settle with Carter. He's a nice guy. You're definitely not going to like what I have to say about it, when I get into the White House." And sure enough, we saw the hostages being released on the morning of Reagan's inauguration.

Of course, the Iranians were aware of Good Guy/Bad Guy, but they didn't want to take a chance that Reagan would follow through with his threats. It demonstrated that these gambits work even when the other side knows what you're doing.

How do you use Good Guy/Bad Guy in salary negotiations? If you are an actor or a sports figure, you would probably have your agent negotiate for you. An agent can position you as the good guy and himself or herself as the bad guy. They can say to the movie producer, "I think my client sees Oscar potential here. But I can't let him work for that kind of money. I'd be the laughingstock of the industry. Once word got out it would ruin his potential for future deals. I'm not even wasting my time taking this kind of offer to him."

There's a good reason why famous people have an agent negotiate their salary for them. The problem for actors and sports personalities is that they don't have much Walk Away Power. They want that role in that movie so much that they're not prepared to walk away. Or they want to play for that team so much that they're not prepared to walk away. I've also found architects very vulnerable in that regard. They have an opportunity to build the building that will define the skyline of their city for generations to come and are not willing to walk away.

If you're in one of those high-profile professions, you'll be much more effective when you can have somebody else negotiating your contract for you. An agent can be much more forceful than you could, and will use Good Guy/Bad Guy very effectively.

Unfortunately, you're probably not in a position where you can have somebody do that for you. You're going to have to do it for yourself. Your Bad Guy has to be your higher authority—your family or your accountant. You say, "I'd love to take what you're offering but I could never sell it to my family. My spouse is going to tell me that our son won't be able to go to college if I take this offer."

Look out for your boss playing Good Guy/Bad Guy with you. In effect he's saying, "Well, if it were up to me I'd give you this increase in pay. But the compensation committee won't approve it." This is simply a subtle form of Good Guy/Bad Guy. The standard counter-gambit to Good Guy/Bad Guy is to recognize what the other person is doing to you. In a light-hearted way you simply laugh it off and say, "Oh come on, Joe, don't play Good Guy/Bad Guy with me on this. We both know that if you really went to bat for me on this you could get me the increase. Now what's stopping you from giving it your full endorsement? Let's get it out on the table."

Counter-Gambits to Good Guy/Bad Guy

- ▷ The first counter-gambit is simply to identify the gambit. Although there are many other ways to handle the problem, this one is so effective that it's probably the only one you need to know. Good Guy/Bad Guy is so well known that it embarrasses people when they are caught using it. When you notice the other person using it you should smile and say, "Oh, come on—you aren't going to play Good Guy/Bad Guy with me are you? Come on, sit down, let's work this thing out." Usually the other side is so embarrassed that they will back off.
- ▷ You could respond by creating a Bad Guy of your own. Tell him or her that you'd love to do what they want, but your family won't go along with it. You can always make a fictitious bad guy appear more unyielding than a bad guy who is present at the negotiation.
- ▷ Sometimes just letting the bad guy talk resolves the problem, especially if he's being obnoxious. Eventually his own people will get tired of hearing it and tell him to knock it off.

- You can counter Good Guy/Bad Guy by saying to the Good Guy, "Look, I understand what you two are doing to me. From now on anything that he says, I'm going to attribute to you also." Now you have two bad guys to deal with, so it diffuses the gambit. Sometimes just identifying them both in your own mind as bad guys will handle it, without you having to come out and accuse them.
- If the other side shows up with an attorney or controller who is clearly there to play bad guy, jump right in and forestall his role. Say to him, "I'm sure you're here to play Bad Guy, but let's not take that approach. I'm as eager to find a solution to this situation as you are, so why don't we all take a win-win approach. Fair enough?" This really takes the wind out of their sails.

Key Points to Consider:

- People use Good Guy/Bad Guy on you much more than you might believe. Look out for it whenever you're negotiating with two or more people.
- It is a very effective way of putting pressure on the other person without creating confrontation.
- Counter it by identifying it. It's such a well-known tactic that when you catch someone using it, he or she gets embarrassed and backs off.
- Don't be concerned that the other side knows what you're doing. Even if he or she does it can still be a powerful tactic. In fact, when you're with an employer who understands all of these gambits, it becomes more fun. Think of it as playing chess with a person of equal skill rather than someone you can easily outsmart.

Chapter 53 ▸▸▸

Taper Down the Size of Your Concessions

In extended negotiations over compensation, be careful that you don't set up a pattern in the way that you make concessions. Let's say that you're negotiating salary and you've gone into the negotiation with a price of $90,000, but you would go as low as $80,000. You have a negotiating range of $10,000.

The way in which you give away that $10,000 is very critical. There are several mistakes that you should avoid:

- Equal-sized concessions.
- Making the final concession a big one.
- Giving it all away up front.
- Giving a small concession to test the waters.

Equal-Sized Concessions

This means giving away your $10,000 negotiating range in four increments of $2,500. Imagine what the employer is thinking if you do that. She doesn't know how far she can push you; all she knows is that every time she pushes she gets another $2,500. She's going to keep on pushing. In fact, it's a mistake to make any two concessions of equal size. If you were hiring someone and the applicant made a $2,500 concession and when pushed made another $2,500 concession, wouldn't you bet that the next concession would be $2,500 also?

Making the Final Concession a Big One

Let's say that you made a $6,000 concession followed by a $4,000 concession. Then you tell the other person, "That's absolutely my bottom line. I won't come down a penny more." The problem is that $4,000 is too big a concession to be your final concession. The other person is probably thinking that you made a $6,000 concession, followed by a $4,000 concession, so he's sure that he can get at least another $1,000 out of you. He says, "We're getting close. If you can come down another $1,000, we can talk." You refuse, telling him that you can't even come down another $100, because you've given him your bottom line already. By now the other person is really upset, because he's thinking, "You just made a $4,000 concession and now you won't give me another lousy $100. Why are you being so difficult?" Avoid making the last concession a big one, because it creates hostility.

Giving It All Away Up Front

Another variation of the pattern is to give the entire $10,000 negotiating range away in one concession. When I set this up as a workshop at my seminars, it's amazing to me how many participants will turn to the person with whom they're to negotiate and say, "Well, I'll tell you what he told me." Such naiveté is a disastrous way to negotiate. I call it "Unilateral Disarmament." It's what some pacifists would have us do about nuclear arms: dismantle all our nuclear weapons and *hope* that the rest of the nuclear powers would reciprocate. I don't think that's very smart.

So you're thinking, "How on earth would a person be able to get me to do a stupid thing like that?" It's easy. You're trying to get hired at a large corporation and the human resources director calls you up and says, "We've narrowed our selection process down to three applicants, so now we're just down to price. We thought the fairest thing to do would be to let all three of you give us your very lowest price, so that we can decide." Unless you're a skilled negotiator, you'll panic and cut your price to the bone, although she hasn't given you any assurance that there won't be another round of bidding later.

Another way that the other side can get you to give away your entire negotiating range up front is with the "we don't like to negotiate" ploy. With a look of pained sincerity on his face, the HR director says, "Let me tell you about the way we do business here. Back in 1926, when he first started the company, our founder said, 'Let's treat our employees well. Let's not negotiate compensation with them. Have them quote their lowest price, and then tell them whether we'll accept it or not.' So that's the way we've always done it. So just give me your lowest price and I'll give you a yes or a no. Because we don't like to negotiate here." The HR director is lying to you. He loves to negotiate. That is negotiating—seeing if you can get the other side to make all of their concessions to you before the negotiating even starts.

Giving a Small Concession to Test the Waters

Giving a small concession first to see what happens tempts us all. You have $10,000 left in your negotiating rage, so you initially tell the employer, "I might be able to settle for $1,000 less, but that's about my limit." If he rejects that, you might think, "This isn't going to be as easy as I thought." So you offer another $2,000. That still doesn't get him to hire you, so in the next round you give away another $3,000, and then you have $4,000 left in your negotiating range, so you give him the whole thing.

You see what you've done there? You started with a small concession and you built up to a larger concession. You'll never reach agreement doing that, because every time he asks you for a concession, it just gets better and better for him.

So all of these are wrong because they create a pattern of expectations in the other person's mind. The best way to make concessions is first to offer a reasonable concession that might just cinch the deal. Maybe a $4,000 concession wouldn't be out of line. Then be sure that if you have to make any future concessions, they're smaller and smaller. Your next concession might be $3,000, and then $2,000, and then $1,000. By reducing the size of the concessions that you're making you convince the other person that he has pushed you about as far as you will go.

If you want to test how effective this can be, try it on your children. Wait until the next time they come to you for money for a school outing. They ask you for $100. You say, "No way. Do you realize that when I was your age my weekly allowance was 50 cents? Out of that, I had to buy my own shoes and walk 10 miles to school in the snow, uphill both ways. So I would take my shoes off and walk barefoot to save money (and other stories that parents the world over tell their children). No way am I going to give you $100. I'll give you $50 and that's it."

"I can't do it on $50," your children protest in horror.

Now you have established the negotiating range. They are asking for $100. You're offering $50. The negotiations progress at a frenzied pace and you move up to $60. Then $65 and finally $67.50. By the time you've reached $67.50, you don't have to tell them that they're not going to do any better. By tapering your concessions, you have subliminally communicated that they're not going to do any better.

Key Points to Consider:

- The way that you make concessions can create a pattern of expectations in the other person's mind.
- Don't make equal-sized concessions, because the other side will keep on pushing.
- Don't make your last concession a big one, because it creates hostility.
- Never concede your entire negotiating range just because the employer calls for your "last and final" proposal or claims that he or she "doesn't like to negotiate."
- Taper the concessions to communicate that the employer is getting the best possible deal.

Chapter 54 ▶▶▶

How to Handle an Impasse

In extended negotiations you will frequently encounter impasses, stalemates, and deadlocks in your employment negotiations. Here's how I define the three terms:

▷ *Impasse*. You are in complete disagreement on one issue (perhaps salary or vacation time) and it threatens the negotiations.

▷ *Stalemate*. Both sides are still talking, but they seem unable to make any progress toward a solution.

▷ *Deadlock*. The lack of progress has frustrated both sides so much that they see no point in talking to each other any more.

It's easy for an inexperienced negotiator to confuse an impasse with a deadlock:

▷ You are $20,000 apart on salary and are beginning to think, "If we're that far apart, it's not going to happen anyway, so why waste any more time on it?"

▷ You got four weeks vacation on your previous job and you have already rented a villa in Italy for your vacation next year. Your potential employer is calling that a deal-breaker, and your family would kill you if you even suggested canceling the trip.

These may sound as though they're deadlocks to the inexperienced negotiator, but to the Power Negotiator, they're only impasses. You can use a very easy gambit whenever you reach an impasse. It's called the Set-Aside Gambit.

The Set-Aside Gambit is what you should use when you're talking to an employer and she says to you, "We might be interested in talking to you, but we have to have you on the job in Houston by the start of the month. If you can't move that quickly, let's not waste time even talking about it."

You are not willing to leave your present employer without giving them two weeks' notice and if you could delay this by two weeks your daughter could graduate from her high school. Even if it's impossible for you to move that quickly, you still use the Set-Aside Gambit: "I understand exactly how important that is to you, but let's just set that aside for a minute and talk about the other issues. Tell me about your healthcare plan. How much vacation do I get the first year? How quickly could we review the compensation?"

When you use the Set-Aside Gambit, you resolve many of the little issues first to establish some momentum in the negotiation before leading up to the big issues. Don't narrow it down to just one issue. (With only one issue on the table, there has to be a winner and there has to be loser.) By resolving the little issues first, you create momentum that will make the big issues much easier to resolve. Inexperienced negotiators always seem to think that you need to resolve the big issues first. "If we can't get together on the major things such as price and terms why waste much time talking to them about the little issues?" Power Negotiators understand the other side will become much more flexible after you've reached agreement on the small issues.

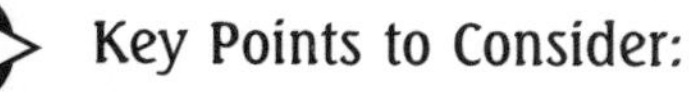

Key Points to Consider:

- Don't confuse an impasse with a deadlock. True deadlocks are very rare, so you've probably reached an impasse.
- Handle an impasse with the Set-Aside Gambit: "Let's just set that aside for a moment and talk about some of the other issues, shall we?"
- Create momentum by resolving minor issues first, but don't narrow the negotiation down to only one issue.

Chapter 55 ▸▸▸
How to Handle a Stalemate

Somewhere between an impasse and a deadlock, you will sometimes encounter a stalemate. That's when both sides are still talking, but seem unable to make any progress toward a solution.

Being in a stalemate is similar to being "in irons," which is a sailing expression meaning that the boat has stalled with its head into the wind. A boat will not sail directly into the wind. It will sail almost into the wind, but it won't sail directly into it. To sail into the wind you must sail about 30 degrees off course to starboard and then tack across the wind 30 degrees to port. It's hard work to keep resetting the sails that way, but eventually you'll get where you want to go. To tack across the wind you must keep the bow of the boat moving smoothly through the wind. If you hesitate you can get stuck with your bow into the wind. If you lose momentum as you tack, there is not enough wind to move the bow of the boat around. When a skipper is "in irons" he or she has to do something to correct the problem—perhaps reset the sails, back up the jib sail to pull the bow around, waggle the tiller or wheel, or do anything that will regain momentum. Similarly, when negotiations stall you must change the dynamics to reestablish momentum. Here are some things that you can do, other than changing the monetary amount involved:

- ▷ Change the people on the negotiating team. A favorite expression that attorneys use is, "I have to be in court this afternoon, so my partner Charlie will be taking my place." The court may be a tennis court, but it's a tactful way of changing the team.

- ▷ Remove a member who may have irritated the other side. A sophisticated negotiator won't take offense at being asked to leave because he or she may have played a valuable role as a Bad Guy. Now it's time to alternate the pressure on the other side by making the concession of removing the person from your team.
- ▷ Change the venue by suggesting that you continue the discussion over lunch or dinner.
- ▷ Ease the tension by talking about the other person's hobbies or a piece of gossip that's in the news or by telling a funny story.
- ▷ Explore the possibility of a change in the way you will be compensated, such as housing allowance, company car, or health club memberships. Any of these may be enough to change the dynamics and move you out of the stalemate.
- ▷ Discuss methods of sharing the risk with the other side. Taking on a commitment that may turn sour might concern them. Try suggesting that one year from now you'll be willing to renegotiate your salary if you don't meet your goals. Perhaps a weasel clause in the contract that applies should the market dramatically change will assuage their fears.
- ▷ Try changing the ambiance in the negotiating room. If the negotiations have been low key with an emphasis on win-win, try becoming more competitive. If the negotiations have been hard-driving, try switching to more of a win-win mode.

- It may be possible to get them to overlook any difference of opinion provided you agree to a method of arbitrating any dispute should it become a problem in the future.

When a sailboat is "in irons" the skipper may know exactly how to reset the sails, but sometimes he or she simply has to try different things to see what works. If negotiations stalemate, you have to try different things to see what will regain momentum for you. Something will happen when you change the dynamics in an attempt to create momentum, but you're never sure what it will be.

Key Points to Consider:

- Be aware of the difference between an impasse, a stalemate, and a deadlock. In a stalemate, both sides still want to find a solution, but neither can see a way to move forward.
- The response to a stalemate should be to change the dynamics of the negotiation by altering one of the elements.

Chapter 56 ▸▸▸

How to Handle a Deadlock

In the previous two chapters, I've shown you how to handle the first two levels of problems that can occur, the impasse and the stalemate. If things get any worse, you may reach a deadlock, something I define as: "Both sides are so frustrated with the lack of progress that they see no point in talking to each other any more."

Deadlocks are rare in salary negotiations, but if you do reach one, the **only** way to resolve it is to bring in a third party—someone who will act as a mediator or arbitrator. There is a major difference between an arbitrator and a mediator. In the case of an arbitrator, both sides agree before the process starts that they will abide by the decision of the arbitrator. If a union critical to the public's welfare goes on strike, such as the union of transportation or sanitation workers, the federal government will eventually insist that an arbitrator be appointed, and both sides will have to settle for the solution that the arbitrator thinks is fair. A mediator doesn't have that kind of power. A mediator is simply someone brought in to facilitate a solution. He or she simply acts as a catalyst, using his or her skills to seek a solution that both sides will accept as reasonable.

Inexperienced negotiators are reluctant to bring in a mediator because they see their inability to resolve a problem as a failure on their part. "I don't want to ask my president for permission to hire a mediator because he'll think of me as a poor negotiator," is what is running through their minds.

Power Negotiators know that there are many reasons why a third party can resolve a problem, other than because they are better negotiators.

An arbitrator or a mediator can be effective only if both sides see him or her as reasonably neutral. Sometimes you must go to great lengths to assure this perception. If you bring in your union representative to resolve a dispute with your employer, what is the chance that your employer will perceive him or her as neutral? Somewhere between nil and zero, right? Your union representative must do something to create a feeling of neutrality in the other person's mind. The way to do this is for your union representative to make a small concession to the employer early in the mediation process.

Your union representative comes in and, even if he's fully aware of the problem, says, "I haven't really had a chance to get into this yet. Why don't you both explain your position and let me see if I can come up with a solution that you can both live with?" The terminology is important here. By asking both sides to explain their positions, he is projecting that he comes to the process without prejudice. Also, note that he's avoiding the use of "we" when he refers to you.

Having patiently heard both sides out, he should then turn to you and say, "Are you being fair pushing that? Perhaps you could give a little on the first-class airfare (or some other detail)? Could you live with coach on flights of less than 90 minutes?" Don't feel that your representative is failing to support you. What he is trying to do is position himself as neutral in your employer's eyes.

Don't assume that you must avoid impasses, stalemates, and deadlocks at all cost. An experienced negotiator can use them as tools to pressure the other side. Once you have it set in your mind that a deadlock is unthinkable, it means that you're no longer willing to walk away, and you have surrendered your most powerful pressure point.

Key Points to Consider:

- The only way to resolve a true deadlock is by bringing in a third party.
- The third party can act as a mediator or an arbitrator. Mediators can only facilitate a solution, but both sides agree up front that they will abide by an arbitrator's final decision.
- Don't see having to bring in a third person as a failure on your part. There are many reasons why third parties can reach a solution that the original parties to the negotiation couldn't reach alone.
- The third party must be seen as neutral by both sides.
- If she is not seen as neutral, she should position herself as such by making a small concession to the other side early in the negotiation.
- Keep an open mind about the possibility of a deadlock. You can only develop your full power as a Power Negotiator if you're willing to walk away. By refusing to consider a deadlock, you're giving away a valuable pressure point.

Chapter 57 ▸▸▸

Positioning for Easy Acceptance

The Positioning for Easy Acceptance Gambit is very important, particularly if you're dealing with an employer who has studied negotiating. If he or she is proud of his ability to negotiate, you can get ridiculously close to agreement, and the entire negotiation will still fall apart on you.

When it does, it's probably not the price or terms of the agreement that caused the problem; it's the ego of the other person as a negotiator. What you may not realize is that just before you showed up in his office, the HR manager said to the president of the company, "You just watch me negotiate with this applicant. I know what I'm doing, and I'll get him or her to accept what we're offering."

Now he's not doing as well as he hoped in the negotiation and he's reluctant to agree to your proposal because he doesn't want to feel that he lost to you as a negotiator. That can happen, even when the HR person knows that your proposal is fair and it satisfies his needs in every way.

When this happens you must find a way to make the employer feel good about giving in to you. You must Position for Easy Acceptance. Power Negotiators know that the best way to do this is to make a small concession just at the last moment. The size of the concession can be ridiculously small, and you can still make it work because it's not the size of the concession that's critical, but the timing.

You might say, "I think the compensation package we talked about is the best I can do, but I'll tell you what. If you'll go along with the package, I'll sit on that ethics committee for you."

Perhaps you were planning to do that anyway, but the point is that you've been courteous enough to position the employer so that he can respond, "Well all right, if you'll do that for me, we'll go along with the package." Then he doesn't feel that he lost to you in the negotiation; he feels that he traded off.

Positioning for Easy Acceptance is another reason why you should never go in with your best offer up front. If you have offered all of your concessions already, before you get to the end of the negotiation, you won't have anything left with which to position the other side.

Here are some other small concessions that you can use to position:

- Offer to author articles for the company newsletter.
- Share your expertise with new employees.
- Represent the company at a service club such as Kiwanis or Lions Club.
- Waive a benefit, such as a new car each year, if you don't meet your performance goals.

Remember that it's the timing of the concession that counts, not the size. The concession can be ridiculously small and still be effective. By using this gambit Power Negotiators can make the other person feel good about giving in to them.

Never, ever gloat. Never, when you get through negotiating, say to the other person, "You know, if you'd hung in there a little big longer, I was prepared to do this and this and this for you."

I realize that in the normal course of business you'd never be foolish enough to gloat over the other person because you felt you out-negotiated him. However, you get into trouble with this one when you're negotiating with someone you know well. Perhaps you've been playing golf with this person for years. Now you're negotiating a compensation package for you to join his company. You both know you're negotiating and you're having fun playing the game. Finally, he says to you, "All right. We're all agreed on this and we're not going to back out, but just for my own satisfaction, what was your real bottom line there?" Of course you are tempted to brag a little, but don't do it. He will remember that for the next 20 years!

Always, when you're through negotiating, offer a congratulations. However poorly you think the other people may have done, congratulate him or her. Say, "Wow. Did you do a fantastic job negotiating with me. I realize that I didn't get as good a deal as I could have done, but frankly, it was worth it because I learned so much about negotiating. You were brilliant." You want the other person to feel that he or she won in the negotiations.

Have you ever watched attorneys in court? They'll cut each other to ribbons inside the courtroom. However, outside in the hallway, you'll see the district attorney go up to the defense attorney and say, "Wow, you were brilliant in there. You really were. It's true that your guy got 30 years, but I don't think anybody could have done a better job than you did." The district attorney understands that he'll be in another courtroom one day with that same defense attorney, and he doesn't want the attorney feeling that this is a personal contest. Gloating over a victory will just make the attorney more determined than ever to win the rematch.

Remember that you will be dealing with that HR director again. You don't want her feeling that she lost to you. It would make her only more determined to get the better of you in a rematch.

Key Points to Consider:

- If the other person is proud of his or her ability to negotiate, his egotistical need to win may stop you from reaching agreement.
- Position the employer to feel good about giving in to you with a small concession made just at the last moment.
- Because timing is more important than the size of the concession, the concession can be ridiculously small and still be effective.
- Always congratulate the other person when you get through negotiating, however poorly you think he or she did.

Chapter 58 ▸▸▸

Nibbling for Your Next Increase

A negotiating gambit that you should always use when applying for an increase in pay or negotiating a compensation package for a new job is Nibbling. The negotiation seems to be over. Everything is agreed upon. But you did appear to give some concessions along the way. Perhaps you asked for 20 percent increase in pay and then settled for a 10 percent increase. Now is an excellent time for you to Nibble for a little bit extra.

Remember the frame of mind of the employer. He's been through a considerable amount of pressure and tension over this negotiation. Finally, an agreement's been reached. You're shaking hands and he's feeling good. When people feel good, they tend to give things away they otherwise wouldn't.

Secondly, when you raise another issue at the very last minute in the negotiation in this way, he tends to think, "Oh no! I thought this was all resolved. I don't want to have to go back through this thing again. Maybe I'm better off to give in on this little issue." This is an excellent time for you to Nibble for something more. It may be that you have a company car that's a couple of years old, and it would be good to say, "Oh, by the way, Joe, it really is time we updated the car I drive, don't you think?" You stand a better chance of getting it then, than at any other time in the negotiation.

Or your Nibble may be for a quick review of this increase in pay. Perhaps your company's policy is to sit down once a year to review an increase in pay. Because you settled for only a 10 percent increase when you deserved a 20 percent increase, perhaps you can say at the last minute, "Joe, look, I was willing to settle for a small increase this time, but don't you think we could review this sooner than next year? Couldn't we sit down and take another look at this six months from now?" You've got a good chance of him going along with something that, if you'd introduced it earlier in the negotiations, he either would deny you or use, as a trade off.

Power Negotiators know that by using the Nibbling Gambit, you can get a little bit more even after you have agreed on everything. You can also get the other person to do things that she had refused to do earlier.

Car salespeople understand this, don't they? They know that when they get you on the lot, a kind of psychological resistance has built up to the purchase. They know to first get you to the point where you're thinking, "Yes, I'm going to buy a car. Yes, I'm going to buy it here"—even if it means closing you on any make and model of car, even a stripped-down model that carries little profit for them. Then they can get you into the closing room and start adding all the other little extras that really build the profit into the car.

The principle of Nibbling tells you that you can accomplish some things more easily with a Nibble later in the negotiations.

Children are brilliant Nibblers, aren't they? If you have teenage children living at home, you know that they don't have to take any courses on negotiating. But you have to—just to stand a chance of surviving the whole process of bringing them up—because they're naturally brilliant negotiators. Not because they learn it in school, but because when they're little everything they get, they get with negotiating skills.

When my daughter, Julia, graduated from high school, she wanted to get a great high school graduation gift from me. She had three things on her hidden agenda.

1. She wanted a five-week trip to Europe.
2. She wanted $1,200 in spending money.
3. She wanted a new set of luggage.

She was smart enough not to ask for everything up front. She was a good enough negotiator to first close me on the trip, then come back a few weeks later and show me in writing that the recommended spending money was $1,200, and she got me to commit to that. Then right at the last minute she came to me and she said, "Dad, you wouldn't want me going to Europe with that ratty old set of luggage, would you? All the kids will be there with new luggage." And she got that, too. Had she asked for everything up front, I would have negotiated out the luggage and negotiated down the spending money.

What's happening here is that a person's mind always works to reinforce decisions that it has just made. Power Negotiators know how this works and use it to get the other side to agree to something that he or she wouldn't have agreed to earlier in the negotiation.

Why is Nibbling such an effective technique? To find out why this works so well, a couple of psychologists did a study at a racetrack in Canada. They studied the attitude of people immediately before they placed the bet and again immediately after they placed the bet. They found out that before the people placed the bet, they were uptight, unsure, and anxious about what they were about to do. Compare this to a potential new employer: They may not know you, they may not know your work, and they certainly don't know what's going to come out of this relationship. Chances are they're uptight, unsure, and anxious.

At the racetrack, the researchers found out that, once people had made the decision to go ahead and place the bet, they suddenly felt very good about what they had just done and even had a tendency to want to double the bet before the race started. In essence, their minds did a flip-flop once they had made the decision. Before they decided, they were fighting it; once they'd made the decision, they supported it.

If you're a gambler, you've had that sensation, haven't you? Watch them at the roulette tables in Atlantic City or Las Vegas. The gamblers place their bets. The croupier spins the ball. At the very last moment, people are pushing out additional bets. The mind always works to reinforce decisions that it has made earlier.

I spoke at a Philadelphia convention when the Pennsylvania lottery prize was $50 million, and many of the people in the audience were holding tickets. To illustrate how people's minds work to reinforce the decisions that they have made, I tried to buy a lottery ticket from somebody in the audience. Do you think he would sell me one? No, he wouldn't, even for fifty times the purchase price. I'm sure that, before he bought that ticket, he was uptight and anxious about betting money on a 100-million-to-one shot. However, having made the decision, he refused to change his mind. The mind works to reinforce decisions that it has made earlier.

So one rule for Power Negotiators is that you don't necessarily ask for everything up front. You wait for a moment of agreement in the negotiations and then go back and Nibble for a little extra.

You might think of the Power Negotiating process as pushing a ball uphill, a large rubber ball that's much bigger than you. You're straining to force it up to the top of the hill. The top of the hill is the moment of first agreement in the negotiations. Once you reach that point, then the ball moves easily down the other side of the hill. This is because people feel good after they have made the initial agreement. They feel a sense of relief that the tension and stress is over. Their minds are working to reinforce the decision they've just made, and they're more receptive to any additional suggestions you may have.

So after the other side has agreed to hire you, it's time for that Second Effort we talked about in the Closing Tactics section. Always go back at the end to make a second effort on something that you couldn't get them to agree to earlier.

Look Out for People Nibbling on You

There's a point in the negotiation when you are very vulnerable, and that point is when you *think* the negotiations are all over.

I bet you've been the victim of a Nibble at one time or another. You've been selling a car or a truck to someone. You're finally feeling good because you've found the buyer. The pressure and the tension of the negotiations have drained away. He's sitting in your office writing out the check. But just as he's about to sign his name he looks up and says, "That does include a full tank of gas, doesn't it?"

You're at your most vulnerable point in the negotiations, for these two reasons:

1. You've just made a sale, and you're feeling good. When you feel good, you tend to give things away that you otherwise wouldn't.
2. You're thinking, "Oh, no. I thought we had resolved everything. I don't want to take a chance on going back to the beginning and re-negotiating the whole thing. If I do that, I might lose the entire sale. Perhaps I'm better off just giving in on this little point."

You're at your most vulnerable when you think the negotiations are over. Look out for employers Nibbling on you.

You're feeling good because you've got the job of your dreams. At the last minute the employer is saying to you, "You do realize, don't you, that the salary is fixed? Any increases are going to be because of the increased business you're bringing in." Because you thought the negotiations were over, and you're afraid to reopen the negotiations for fear of losing the opportunity completely, you will be very tempted to take the deal.

Countering the Nibble When the Employer Does It to You

The Counter Gambit to the Nibble is to gently make the other person feel cheap. You have to be very careful about the way you do this because obviously you're at a sensitive point in the negotiation. You smile sweetly and say: "Oh, come on, you negotiated a fantastic package with me. Don't make me waive any increases, too. Fair enough?" That's the Counter Gambit to the Nibble when it's used against you. Be sure that you do it with a big grin on your face, so that the other person doesn't take it too seriously.

Consider these points when you go into negotiations:

- ▷ Are there some elements that you are better off to bring up as a Nibble, after you have reached initial agreement? Perhaps it's easier to get that company car or country club membership after you've reached agreement on the balance of the package.
- ▷ Do you have a plan to make a second effort on anything to which you can't get them to agree the first time around?
- ▷ Are you prepared for the possibility of them Nibbling on you at the last moment?

You can avoid most of this unpleasantness by:

- Negotiating all the details up front and getting them in writing. Don't leave anything to "we can work that out later." Don't be lazy and feel that if you avoid an issue you are closer to sealing the deal.
- Use the Gambits to create a climate in which the other person feels that he or she won. If she felt that she won, then she is much less likely to Nibble—either during the negotiation or afterward.

Power Negotiators always take into account the possibility of being able to Nibble. Timing is very critical—catching the other party when the tension is off and they're feeling good because they think the negotiations are all over.

On the other hand, looking out for the other side Nibbling on you at the last moment, when you're feeling good. At that point, you're the most vulnerable and liable to make a concession that half an hour later you'll be thinking, "Why on earth did I do that? I didn't have to do that. We'd agreed on everything already."

Key Points to Consider:

- With a well-timed Nibble, you can get things at the end of a negotiation that you couldn't have gotten the other side to agree to earlier.
- It works because the other person's mind reverses itself after it has made a decision. He or she may have been fighting the thought of paying so much you at the start of the negotiation. After he or she has made a decision to hire you, however, you can Nibble for a larger office, better car, or additional benefits.
- Being willing to make that additional effort is what separates great people from merely good people.

- When the other person Nibbles on you, respond by making him or her feel cheap, in a good-natured way.
- Avoid post-negotiation Nibbling by addressing and tying up all the details and using Gambits that cause the other negotiator to feel as if he or she has won.

Chapter 59 ▸▸▸

Let's Make This Win-Win

Let's talk about win-win negotiating. Instead of using negotiating tactics to get your boss to do something he wouldn't normally do, I believe that you should work with your boss to work out your problems and develop a solution with which both of you can win.

Your reaction to that may be, "Roger, you obviously don't know much about my industry. I live in a dog-eat-dog world. There's no such thing as win-win at my organization. They just want the most amount of work for the least amount of money. How on earth can we both win?"

Let's start out with the most important issue: What do we mean when we say win-win? Does it really mean that both sides win? Or does it mean that both sides lose equally so that it's fair? What if each side thinks that they won and the other side lost—would that be win-win?

Before you dismiss that possibility, think about it more. What if you leave the salary negotiation thinking, "I won. I would have taken less if my boss had been a better negotiator"? However, your boss is thinking that she won and that she would have given you more if you had been a better negotiator. So both of you think that you won and the other person lost. Is that win-win? Yes, I believe it is, as long as it's a permanent feeling. As long as neither of you wake up tomorrow morning thinking, "Son of a gun, now I know what she did to me. Wait until I see her again."

That's why I stress doing things that service the perception that the other side won, such as:

- ▷ Don't jump at the first offer.
- ▷ Ask for more than you expect to get.
- ▷ Flinch at the other side's proposals.
- ▷ Avoid confrontation.
- ▷ Use the Vise Gambit: You'll have to do better than that.
- ▷ Use Higher Authority and Good Guy/Bad Guy to make the other person think you're on his or her side.
- ▷ Never offer to split the difference.
- ▷ Set aside impasse issues.
- ▷ Always ask for a trade-off and never make a concession without a reciprocal concession.
- ▷ Taper down your concessions.
- ▷ Position the other side for easy acceptance.

Besides constantly servicing the perceptions that the other side won, observe these four fundamental rules of win-win negotiating:

- ▷ Don't narrow it down to just one issue.
- ▷ People are not out for the same thing.
- ▷ Don't try to get the last dollar off the table.
- ▷ Put something back on the table.

Don't Narrow It Down to Just One Issue

The first thing to learn is this: Don't narrow the negotiation down to just one issue. If, for example, you resolve all the other issues and the only thing left to negotiate is your pay, somebody has to win and somebody has to lose. As long as you keep more than one issue on the table, you can always work trade-offs so that the other person doesn't mind conceding on salary because you are able to offer something in return.

You should do what you can to put other issues, such as vacations, profit sharing, health benefits, and car allowance onto the table so that you can use these items for trade-offs and get away from the perception that this is a one-issue negotiation.

In a one-issue negotiation, you should add other elements so that you can trade them off later and appear to be making concessions. If you find yourself deadlocked with a one-issue negotiation, you should try adding other issues into the mix. Fortunately, usually many more elements than just the one main issue are important in negotiations. The art of win-win negotiating is to piece together those elements the way one puts together a jigsaw puzzle, so that both people can win. Rule one is this: Don't narrow the negotiations down to just one issue. Though we may resolve impasses by finding a common ground on small issues to keep the negotiation moving, you should never narrow it down to one issue.

People Are Not Out for the Same Thing

Rule number two that makes you a win-win negotiator is the understanding that people are not out for the same thing. We all have an overriding tendency to assume that other people want what we want, and because of this we believe that what's important to us will be important to them. But that's not true.

The biggest trap into which neophyte negotiators fall is assuming that price is the dominant issue in a negotiation. Many other elements, other than salary, are important to your boss:

- ▷ Will this be difficult to sell to your boss's boss?
- ▷ Will you still be an enthusiastic employee if the company gives you less than you ask for?
- ▷ Will this create a precedent that other employees will expect?

These all come into play, along with half a dozen other factors. The second key to win-win negotiating is this: Don't assume that they want what you want. Because if you do, you further make the assumption that anything you do in the negotiations to help them get what they want helps them and hurts you.

Win-win negotiating can come about only when you understand that people don't want the same things in the negotiation. So Power Negotiating becomes not just a matter of getting what you want, but also being concerned about the other person getting what he or she wants. One of the most powerful thoughts you can have when you're negotiating with someone is not "What can I get from them?" but "What can I give them that won't take away from my position?" Because when you give people what they want, they will give you what you want in a negotiation.

Don't Try to Get the Last Dollar off the Table

The third key to win-win negotiating is this: Don't be too greedy. Don't try to get the last dollar off the table. You may feel that you triumphed, but does that help you if the other person felt that you vanquished him? That last dollar left on the table is a very expensive dollar to pick up.

Don't try to get it all; leave something on the table so that the other person feels that she won also.

Put Something Back on the Table

The fourth key to win-win negotiating is this: Put something back on the table when the negotiation is over. I don't mean by telling him or her that you'll take less than what you negotiated. I mean do something more than you promised to do. Perhaps you tell him, "Be sure and let me know if you want me to fill in for you at that orientation session you teach." You'll find that the little extra for which he didn't have to negotiate means more to him than everything for which he did have to negotiate.

Key Points to Consider:

- Look at it from their point of view, not yours. What you would do if you were them has absolutely nothing to do with it.
- Different people have different goals, relationships, styles, faults, and different methods of getting what they want.
- Winning is a perception, and by constantly servicing the perception that the other person is winning you can convince him that he has won without having to make any concessions to him.
- Don't narrow the negotiation down to just one issue.
- Don't assume that helping the other person get what he or she wants takes away from your position. You're not out for the same thing. Poor negotiators try to force the other person to get off the positions that he or she has taken. Power negotiators know that even when positions are 180 degrees apart, the interests of both sides can be identical, so they work to get people off their positions and concentrating on their interests.
- Don't be greedy. Don't try to get the last dollar off the table.
- Put something back on the table. Do more than you bargained for.

Index

About the Author

Roger Dawson was born in England, immigrated to California in 1962, and became a United States citizen 10 years later. Formerly the president of one of California's largest real estate companies, he became a full-time author and professional speaker in 1982.

His Nightingale-Conant audio program *Secrets of Power Negotiating* is the largest-selling business cassette program ever published. Four of his books have been main selections of major book clubs.

Roger Dawson is the founder of The Power Negotiating Institute, a California-based organization (*www.rdawson.com*).

Companies and associations throughout North America and around the world call on him for his expertise in negotiation, persuasion, and decision-making, and for motivational keynote speeches. His seminar company (The Power Negotiating Institute, 1045 East Road, La Habra Heights, CA 90631, USA; Tel. 800-YDAWSON [932-9766]) conducts seminars on Power Negotiating, Power Persuasion, Confident Decision Making, and High Achievement around the world. Roger was inducted into the Speakers Hall of Fame in 1992.

***Please contact Roger Dawson with any suggestions, criticisms, or questions by e-mailing him at* RogDawson@aol.com. *His Website address is* www.rdawson.com.**

Also by Roger Dawson

Books

Secrets of Power Negotiating

Secrets of Power Negotiating for Salespeople

Secrets of Power Persuasion

Secrets of Power Persuasion for Salespeople

The Confident Decision Maker

The 13 Secrets of Power Performance

With Mike Summey

The Weekend Millionaire's Secrets to Investing in Real Estate

Weekend Millionaire Mindset

The Weekend Millionaire's Frequently Asked Questions

Audio Programs

Secrets of Power Negotiating

Secrets of Power Persuasion

Secrets of Power Performance

Confident Decision Making

The Personality of Achievers

Secrets of Power Negotiating for Salespeople

With Mike Summey

The Weekend Millionaire's Real Estate Investing Program

Video Training Programs

Guide to Everyday Negotiating

Guide to Business Negotiating

Guide to Advanced Negotiating

Power Negotiating for Salespeople (a 12-part series)

Speeches and Seminars by Roger Dawson

If you hire speakers for your company or influence the selection of speakers at your association, you should learn more about Roger Dawson's speeches and seminars. He will customize his presentation to your company or industry so that you get a unique presentation tailored to your needs.

Roger Dawson's presentations include:

- ▷ Secrets of Power Negotiating
- ▷ Secrets of Power Persuasion
- ▷ Confident Decision Making
- ▷ The 13 Secrets of Power Performance

To get more information and receive a complimentary press kit, please call, write, e-mail, or fax:

The Power Negotiating Institute
214 San Carlos Way
Placentia, CA 92870 USA
Phone: (800) YDAWSON (932–9766)
Fax: (714) 993–2580
E-mail: *Dawsonprod@aol.com*
Website: *rdawson.com*

Roger Dawson's audio programs and videocassette albums are available from:

The Power Negotiating Institute
214 San Carlos Way
Placentia, CA 92870 USA

You can order by calling (800) YDAWSON (932–9766), by e-mailing *DawsonProd@aol.com.* or by faxing (714) 993–2580.

Audio Programs

Secrets of Power Negotiating

Six-CD audio album with workbook and 24 flash cards. $69.95

This is one of the largest-selling business audio albums ever published, with sales of more than $28 million. You'll learn 20 powerful negotiating gambits that are surefire winners. Then, going beyond the mere mechanics of the negotiating process, Roger Dawson helps you learn what influences people, and how to recognize and adjust to different negotiating styles, so you can get what you want regardless of the situation.

Also, you'll learn:

- ▷ A new way of pressuring people without confrontation.
- ▷ The one unconscious decision you must never make in a negotiation.
- ▷ The five standards by which every negotiation should be judged.
- ▷ Why saying yes too soon is always a mistake.
- ▷ How to gather the information you need without the other side knowing.
- ▷ The three stages that terrorist negotiators use to defuse crisis situations.
- ▷ And much, much more.

Secrets of Power Negotiating for Salespeople

Six-CD audio album. $69.95

This program, which supplements and enhances Roger Dawson's famous generic negotiating program *The Secrets of Power Negotiating*, teaches salespeople how to negotiate with buyers and get higher prices without having to give away freight and terms. It's the most in-depth program ever created for selling at higher prices than your competition and still maintaining long-term relationships with your customers. It's guaranteed to dramatically improve your profit margins or we'll give your money back.

Special Offer. Invest in both Secrets of Power Negotiating and Secrets of Power Negotiating for Salespeople and save $20. Both for only $120.

Secrets of Power Persuasion

Six-CD audio album. $69.95

In this remarkable program, Roger Dawson shows you the strategies and tactics that will enable you to persuade people in virtually any situation. Not by using threats or phony promises, but because they perceive that it's in their best interest to do what you say.

You'll discover why *credibility* and above all *consistency* are the cornerstones of getting what you want. You'll learn verbal persuasion techniques that defuse resistance and demonstrate the validity of your thinking. Step by step, you'll learn to develop an overwhelming aura of personal *charisma* that will naturally cause people to like you, respect you, and to gladly agree with you. It's just a matter of mastering the specific, practical behavioral techniques that Roger Dawson presents in a highly entertaining manner.

Secrets of Power Performance

Six-CD audio album. $69.95

With this program, you'll learn how to get the best from yourself—and those around you! Roger Dawson firmly believes that we are all capable of doing so much more than we think we're capable of. Isn't that true for you? Aren't you doing far more now than you thought you could do five years ago? With the life-changing secrets revealed in this best selling program, you'll be able to transform your world in the next five years!

Confident Decision Making

Six-CD audio album, with 36-page workbook.
$69.95

Decisions are the building blocks of your life. The decisions you've made have given you everything you now have. The decisions you'll make from this point on will be responsible for everything that happens to you for the rest of your life. Wouldn't it be wonderful to know that, from this point on, you'll always be making the right choice? All you have to do is listen to this landmark program.

You'll learn:

- ▷ How to quickly and accurately categorize your decision.
- ▷ How to expand your options with a ten-step creative thinking process.
- ▷ How to find the right answer with reaction tables and determination trees.
- ▷ How to harness the power of synergism with the principle of Huddling.
- ▷ How to know exactly what and how your boss, customer, or employee will decide.
- ▷ And dozens more powerful techniques.

Beyond Goals—The Personality of Achievers

Six-cassette audio album. $69.95

You can learn how to go beyond your most ambitious goals with this breakthrough program. Life's high achievers know that there is no substitute for action—the positive, disciplined transformations of thoughts into deeds. This program identifies what makes people high achievers and shows you what—and how—these super-successful people think, how they act, and how they inspire others to help them succeed. It contains fascinating studies of personalities and behavior and transforms them into practical, common sense strategies that will lead you to uncommon success.

Video Training Programs

Guide to Business Negotiations

One-hour VHS video. $79.95

Guide to Everyday Negotiations

One-hour VHS video. $89.95

Guide to Advance Negotiations

One-hour VHS video. $89.95

Special price: Set of all three video programs for just $149.

If you're in any way responsible for training or supervising other people, these videos will liven up your staff meetings and turn your people into master negotiators. Your sales and profits will soar, as you build new win-win relationships with your customers and clients. Then use these programs to develop a training library for your employees' review, and for training new hires.